ENGLISH
WINE

ENGLISH WINE

YOUR ESSENTIAL COMPANION, FROM VINE TO WINE

SAM CAPORN

Illustrations by Claire Littlejohn

BLOOMSBURY PUBLISHING
LONDON • OXFORD • NEW YORK • NEW DELHI • SYDNEY

BLOOMSBURY PUBLISHING
Bloomsbury Publishing Plc
50 Bedford Square, London, WC1B 3DP, UK
29 Earlsfort Terrace, Dublin 2, DO2 AY28, Ireland

BLOOMSBURY, BLOOMSBURY PUBLISHING and the Diana logo are trademarks of Bloomsbury Publishing Plc

First published in Great Britain 2026

A catalogue record for this book is available from the British Library

Library of Congress Cataloguing-in-Publication data has been applied for

ISBN: HB: 978-1-0372-0752-5; eBook: 978-1-0372-0753-2

10 9 8 7 6 5 4 3 2 1

Designed by Luke Bird
Cover designed by Carmen Balit

Printed and bound in Great Britain by Clays Ltd, Elcograf S.p.A

MIX
Paper | Supporting responsible forestry
FSC® C018072

To find out more about our authors and books visit www.bloomsbury.com and sign up for our newsletters. For product-safety related questions contact productsafety@bloomsbury.com

For Ed & Wilf
The grain to my grape

Contents

Welcome

First of all, let me say what a lot of fun this book has been to research and write! Following a couple of requests from friends, keen for my advice on which English vineyards they should visit, I realised, to my surprise, that no book existed on the subject. There was nothing that covered what you could expect at different wineries: if tours and tastings were offered, whether you could eat or stay there and, of course, crucially, what the wines were like – in essence the 'experience'. And from that initial seed, the idea for this book came into fruition, a book for everyone and anyone who enjoys a glass of wine (possibly the only prerequisite), from total newbies to bona fide wine buffs.

The book is divided into two sections, and the first provides a helpful overview and some context on English wine, including its history, thoughts on wine styles, practical tips for your visit, and a handy 'wine word' glossary. Back in 2011 I wrote my Master of Wine dissertation on English sparkling wine, and the growth and dynamism that has occurred since then is nothing short of staggering. The days of being fairly one-dimensional and only making superlative, traditional method sparkling wines are no more – though these world-beating bottles of bubbles are still being made. Instead, there is a wealth of different grapes and wine styles out there waiting to be discovered, from hybrids and PIWIs to Charmat, Pét-Nat, skin-contact, elegant whites and crunchy reds. This is such a fun, vibrant and eclectic industry that isn't governed by many rules and regulations and, as such, is free to play around and experiment.

The second section of the book takes you with me on a journey of discovery. I visited over seventy different vineyards and wineries, most of which are situated in the south of the country; a remarkable 65 per cent or so of plantings are in the South East alone, notably in Kent and Sussex. Slightly warmer temperatures and longer sunshine hours make a real difference to grape ripening in relatively marginal climates, and the rich seams of chalk soils are geologically the same as those in Champagne: ideal for those looking to make sparkling wines. I was also looking for a range of wineries, experiences and wine styles, from destination wineries with remarkable restaurants to boutique wine hotels, award-winning and urban wineries, or small family-run concerns and pioneer producers.

What became really clear on my travels was that there is a quiet revolution going on, not just in the vineyard and winery but also with regards to hospitality. Gone are the plethora of modest cellar doors (typically a small shop and/or tasting space) and in their place are a raft of enticing experiences, events and eateries, encouraging visitors to set off for England's Elysian vineyards to taste some of their first-rate wines. It's also possible to visit 'clusters' of wineries or take part in an organised tour to really experience and explore what England has to offer. And the wine-curious amongst us don't even have to dig out a passport or jump on a plane in order to be able to do this: to wander between the vines or enjoy an al fresco lunch. This book is intended to encourage and help all wine lovers to get out there and explore our exceptional English offering: there is simply nothing better than tasting wines where they are made, understanding the challenges faced, and supporting our exciting industry. So, what are you waiting for? Let's go wine tasting!

Part One

All You Need to Know About English Wine

A (Very) Brief History

England, quite understandably, has a reputation for being wet and cold, so, consequently, it was largely rot-resistant Germanic grape varieties, usually hybrids, that were originally planted by the pioneering producers of the 1970s, the first real risk-takers who laid the foundations for all those who followed in their footsteps. But when Stuart and Sandy Moss – the 'can do' couple from Chicago, USA – bought Nyetimber, they didn't want to plant those old-fashioned varieties and so, against all advice and prevailing wisdom, they turned to the classic French Champagne varieties (Chardonnay, Pinot Noir and Pinot Meunier), which ultimately heralded a new era or renaissance for England: the making of world-class sparkling wines. Today there exists a happy balance between the two, along with the more experimental, low-intervention, 'new-wave' winemakers crafting a range of different wines and styles.

THE ORIGIN STORY

1952
Hambledon Vineyard, Hampshire is the first commercial vineyard planted

THE PIONEERING PRODUCERS

1969
The Barnes family establish vines at Biddenden in Kent

1972
Bolney Wine Estate (then Bookers Vineyard) plant vines in West Sussex

1974
Breaky Bottom follows suit in East Sussex

THE NYETIMBER EFFECT

1988
Nyetimber plant Chardonnay, Pinot Noir and Pinot Meunier for sparkling wines

1995
Ridgeview follow fairly soon afterwards, with the industry really now starting to evolve, appealing to many an entrepreneur with deep pockets

2002
Balfour plant their first five acres

2010
Mark and Sarah Driver buy Rathfinny

THE NEW-WAVE WINEMAKER

2017
Adrian Pike starts at Westwell

2018
The first vines are planted at Tillingham

2020
Sharpham Estate moves to Sandridge Barton

English sparkling wine – more than just a Champagne copycat

Nyetimber indisputably put England on the wine map with the release of their very first award-winning wine, and the ensuing plaudits and press caught the eye of many an entrepreneur. This seemingly inspired others, as since the 1990s there has been a massive increase in the number of vineyards being planted in England. Ridgeview in Sussex was established in 1995, just after Nyetimber, and since then, the south of the country in particular has seen monumental growth, due to the combination of a slightly warmer climate and those chalky soils. Interestingly, some Champagne houses have even been getting in on the act with both Taittinger – Domaine Evremond in Kent – and Pommery (Louis Pommery England, Hampshire) planting vines in 2017.

But English sparkling wine isn't just a Champagne copycat. The wines are arguably fresher and brisker with a line of citrus acidity, and whilst they aren't exactly Prosecco prices – small volumes, expensive land and costly winemaking means prices can be on the high side – a vintage English sparkling wine tends to be better value than a non-vintage Champagne and significantly so when compared to a vintage Champagne.

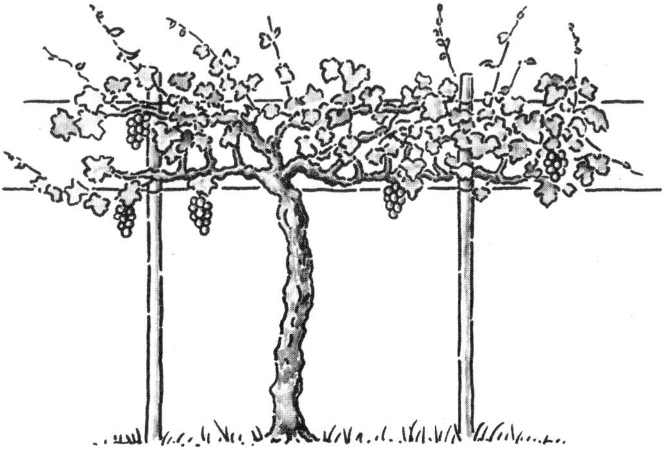

Oak is the Way Forward

This even tends to be the case when an English sparkling wine has had some 'oak influence' – which tends to make wine more expensive. This is when a portion of the base still wine is fermented and/or aged in oak for a period of time, and once it goes through its second fermentation, the flavours resemble spiced crumble and apple Danish. The spice is usually subtle and well integrated but helps moderate acidity and allows for enhanced complexity and ageing potential. England's superb still wines – from Pinot Gris, *flor*-style whites, Chardonnay, Pinot Noir, Cabaret Noir and Rondo – can also benefit from time spent in oak with even some Bacchus (typically aromatic and fresh) sometimes seeing a smidgen.

The rise of rosé

Plaudits for English sparkling rosé have been coming in thick and fast ever since they first came onto the market and again, compared to the price of pink Champagne, they look like pretty good value. But what is special about these wines is that they are so refreshing, crunchy (pleasantly tart) and characterful. Whilst the red berry fruit flavours can be hidden by the autolysis in many a Champagne, here they are really allowed to sing, resulting in wines that are redolent of raspberry pip, strawberry and cranberry. These are some of the very best wines this country has to offer, and still wines are finally getting in on the act too. Pale and dry with delicate notes of berries and blossom, they are largely the same price as Provençal pinks but from smaller, often family-owned concerns rather than massive behemoths.

The (re)emergence of excellent still wines

Ever since Nyetimber burst onto the English wine scene, the focus of the industry has largely been on these first-rate fizzes. But change is afoot and as our climate continues to get warmer the still wines just keep on getting better – nowhere is this more true than with regards to the fruit coming out of the Crouch Valley in Essex and Kit's Coty in Kent. Classic French varieties such as Chardonnay and Pinot Noir are shining but, interestingly, there is also a new wave of winemaker returning to our viticultural roots and making delicious wines from our old friends the Germanic hybrids and also PIWIs. Add in an interest in low intervention, oxidative handling (including *flor*) and experimentation with the use of vessels such as qvevri, the wines now being made in England are as distinctive and delicious as they have ever been.

The power of PIWIs and the strength of sustainability

Sustainable practices (audited by Sustainable Wines of Great Britain or SWGB) and regenerative viticulture are both widespread in England but there aren't actually many organic or biodynamic producers: mainly Albury, Davenport, Limeburn Hill, Oxney, Sedlescombe and Tillingham. This is because our rainy climate means that rot is a very real risk and can decimate a crop, so spraying is typically required to contain or control it, and options are more limited for those who are organic. However, for producers who want to limit their reliance on sprays without converting to organics, there is another option; planting PIWI varietals. A German acronym for *Pilzwiderstandsfähig*, this translates as 'fungus-resistant' and as such they massively mitigate against the need to protect against the likes of powdery and downy mildew. Look out for names such as Sauvignac, Seyval Blanc, Solaris and Souvignier Gris for whites and Cabaret Noir, Divico, Regent and Rondo for reds. They might not be instantly recognisable yet, but they may very well be the future of still wines.

Practical Tips

Here are my top tips to get the most out of your winery visits; most importantly, though, do plan ahead and book tours and tastings in advance.

Opening hours: These vary widely depending on the winery and season, so do check in advance.

Online bookings: Self-guided tastings don't require a booking, but for guided tours or tastings, check online for availability and be sure to secure your spot. Ditto for a restaurant table or a specific event.

Organised tours: Look out for companies who arrange wine trips, such as Great British Wine Tours, Shuttle & Vine and Vine + Country Wine Tours.

Accessibility: Many wineries, restaurants and cellar doors are wheelchair accessible, but vineyards largely are not, due to the uneven terrain, although Leonardslee takes guests out to the vines in golf buggies.

Dogs: Typically, dogs are not allowed on the tours but are often welcome elsewhere on the estate, including in restaurants.

Children: Most tours are for 18+, but children are usually welcome on site.

Taxis: Vineyards tend to be in the country and 99 per cent of the time there is no Uber available, but local taxis can be booked.

Clusters: Increasingly, wineries are grouping into 'clusters' to help visitors plan their trips: in Kent there is the Wine Garden of England, Vineyards of Hampshire, Vineyards of the Surrey Hills, the Wealden Wine Trail, the Rother Wine Triangle from Sussex Wine-lands and, most recently, there are plans to create an Arun and Adur Wine Valley 'collective'.

English Wine Week: Annually in June, this is a great time to visit, with additional activities often running.

Gifting: Winery visits make great gifts and vouchers for visits (and/or wine) are easy both to purchase and redeem; typically within a year.

Staying: With a range of accommodation options either available onsite or nearby, it is absolutely worth thinking about making a weekend of it.

How to Use This Book

There are over seventy vineyards and/or wineries to explore in this book and they are organised by the wider, larger region first, of which there are four: the South East, the South West, East Anglia and London, and then divided further by county and, finally, alphabetically.

Within each separate winery entry, you will find a backstory to help you get to know the people behind the wines, some tasting notes and practical information on tours, restaurants and accommodation. These frequently detail nearby wineries, highlighting which others are in the vicinity, for those keen to visit as many as possible over the course of a day, weekend or even a week. There are also a handful of 'add on' wineries that I felt deserved more than a passing mention, so watch out for those on pages 39, 55, 65, 66, 69, 97, 168 and 183.

Finally, the toothsome wines tasted were both non-vintage and vintage. The exact vintages sipped are not specified in the tasting notes and thus they are intended to provide an indication of flavour only. Still wines are noted with +, and * next to the wine indicates one of my top picks. There is also a price guide, which is the same for both still and sparkling:

<£20	£
£21–30	££
£31–40	£££
£41–50	££££
£50+	£££££
£100+	££££££

Prices reflect the boutique nature of production (quantities made are often modest), that making traditional method sparkling wine is expensive, and that wine quality is often extraordinary, with many wines being highly awarded. The main competitions in England are Decanter World Wine Awards (DWWA), WineGB Awards, the International Wine Challenge (IWC) and the International Wine & Spirit Competition (IWSC). Smaller regional competitions also exist, but many of the larger ones remain integral in catapulting producers into global recognition, and providing column inches and opportunities.

How to Taste Wine

Whether you are enjoying a self-guided tasting or are being taken through a selection of wines as part of a tour and tasting, here are a few tips to help get the most out of your glass.

Hold your glass by the stem: this makes it easier to swirl but also keeps fizz, white or rosé cool for longer.

Look at the wine: the depth of colour tells you a lot about what you can expect from a wine. As a rule of thumb, the deeper the colour, the more flavourful and structured the wine is likely to be. Also with fizz, look at the bubbles. Are they small and rising fast (better quality) or slower and bigger – more likely to be made using the Charmat (or tank) method?

Swirl the wine: this releases the 'volatile aromatics', which are hugely important, as you don't really taste wine, you smell it, and so this is an integral part of wine 'tasting'. You can only taste sweet, salty, bitter, sour and umami, and it is when aroma and taste combine that you get flavour.

Smell the wine: identifying aromas is tricky, but I've popped tasting notes throughout the book to guide you.

Taste the wine: the really fun bit and, even better, you aren't expected to spit! As well as trying to identify flavour – although the most important part is deciding how much you like it – also consider structure. Is the wine light, medium or full-bodied? What is the acidity like, or is there oak?

Wine Word Glossary

Whilst visiting your vineyard and/or winery, you are very likely to come across a number of wine words that are unfamiliar to you. I've detailed some important ones below, but if something comes up that isn't here, then do ask. The tour guides typically love a question, are wine-qualified, and will be delighted to help.

Amphora: A porous, inert winemaking vessel, typically made from terracotta.

Assemblage: Blending.

Biodynamic: Very holistic, taking into account phases of the moon and using special preparations.

Blanc de Blancs: Sparkling wine made from white grapes (Chardonnay typically) only. Tend to be more elegant and poised.

Blanc de Noirs: Sparkling wine made from red grapes only (though still white in colour), usually Pinot Noir and Pinot Meunier. Tend to be a bit more structured than Blanc de Blancs.

Charmat: Also known as the tank method, this is when the second fermentation to create the fizz takes place in a tank, resulting in less complex, fruitier wines (also cheaper).

Clone: When a grape variety is propagated (for example, by taking cuttings) after showing beneficial attributes: Chardonnay has many clones, such as Mendoza, Gingin, 76 and 95, but they are all still Chardonnay.

Col Fondo: An Italian term when the wine undergoes a second fermentation in the bottle (unlike Pét-Nat, which only has one) but is not disgorged, resulting in some haze and sediment.

Cross: A new variety created from crossing two of the same species (usually *Vitis vinifera*, the main grape vine species).

Demi-Sec: a medium-sweet sparkling wine with residual sugar levels of between 32–50 grams per litre. Brut, for context, is 0–12 g/l RS.

Disgorging: Removing the yeast lees (or plug) from traditional method sparkling wine.

Dosage: After disgorging, some liquid is lost and so a mix of wine and sugar is added to 'top up' and balance acidity.

Fining: See Unfiltered/unfined.

Flor: A layer of yeast that can develop on wine during ageing which gives savoury, nutty notes.

Gravity-fed: A premium, more gentle way of handling wine, using gravity (height) to move wine around rather than pumps.

Great British Classic Method: Essentially a marketing term, rather than a legal requirement, denoting the need for a minimum of nine months on lees.

Hybrid: A new variety created from different *Vitis* species (for example, *Vitis vinifera*, *Vitis labrusca* or *riparia*). Seyval Blanc is a French-American hybrid and a PIWI.

Lees ageing (also yeast autolysis): The crux of the traditional method; the contact of the sparkling wine with the dead yeast results in the desirable bakery and bready notes.

Low/minimal intervention: A hands-off approach, where you make wine as naturally as possible.

MLF: Short for malolactic fermentation; a bacterial conversion when malic acid (think apples) is converted to softer lactic acid (think milk), resulting in a smoother, more rounded wine.

Mousse: The bubbles or fizz.

MV: Meaning multi-vintage, this is often used instead of NV or non-vintage, but is the same thing.

NV: Non-vintage means a wine that is made from the grapes of more than one specific year or vintage.

Orange or amber wine/skin contact: When the fermenting or fermented wine spends time in contact with the (white) grape skins, resulting in more colour, flavour and texture.

PDO Sussex: Meaning 'protected designation of origin' (a European Union initiative – think Parmesan and feta). For still and sparkling wines, with the sparkling requiring a minimum of fifteen months in bottle, with at least twelve on the lees, whereas PDO England needs only nine months on lees.

Pét-Nat: Short for *pétillant naturel* (or *méthode ancestrale*), when the wine is bottled before the first fermentation has finished, so there is no need to add yeast and sugar.

Pinot Noir Précoce: An early-ripening clone of Pinot Noir.

PIWI: This German term, short for *Pilzwiderstandsfähig*, means fungus-resistant (grape varieties), so less spraying is needed, making them more sustainable.

Plumpton College: Offering wine-based (amongst others) undergraduate degrees, diplomas and courses in East Sussex.

Qvevri: A Georgian winemaking clay vessel or amphora.

Regenerative viticulture: Placing great importance on soil health and biodiversity; the antithesis of intensive farming.

Reserve wines: When base wines – the fairly neutral still wines intended to become sparkling – from previous years are kept back or 'in reserve' to enhance complexity when blended with younger wines, and also to provide consistency of style.

Rootstocks: The vine is grafted onto a phylloxera- (devastating vineyard insect) resistant root, or rootstock with other benefits offered too, for example, suitability for specific soils.

Sabrage: Removing the cork from a sparkling wine using a sword or knife.

Sulphur dioxide (SO_2): A wine byproduct and preservative often erroneously blamed for headaches.

Tannins: Found in grape skins, seeds and stems, they are vital for wine structure and ageing. Also responsible for the drying sensation felt at the sides of the mouth when drinking, mainly in red wines but also in some skin-contact or orange wines.

Terroir: A French term meaning a 'sense of place'; the soils, aspect and microclimate, mainly.

Traditional method: When the second fermentation to create the fizz takes place in a bottle, resulting in more savoury, yeasty, complex wines.

Unfiltered/unfined (vegan): Most commercial wines are fined and filtered to make them clean and bright, but it can strip some personality from the wine. Fining agents can include albumin (egg white) and isinglass (a fish derivative), so no fining agents means the wine is vegan, though bentonite is a vegan alternative.

Vintage: When a wine is made from one specific year, the one in which the fruit was picked and which is shown on the bottle. Climatic conditions lead to vintage variation, with some vintages being better than others, depending on the weather conditions during specific stages such as flowering, fruit set, the growing season and harvest.

Wild fermentation: A fermention that uses naturally occurring wild yeasts (see below).

Wild yeasts: Typically, cultured yeasts are used for fermentation, as wild yeasts are more unpredictable, but they result in greater complexity.

Part Two

The Wineries

Wherever you live and whatever you are looking for in a vineyard visit (or visits), there is a winery out there for everyone and for every occasion. Whether you are planning a romantic weekend away, a girls' day out (or hen do), a birthday celebration, corporate event, wedding reception, or lunch with a friend or family member with a delicious glass of wine and want to learn more about the styles that you enjoy, then look no further than an English winery.

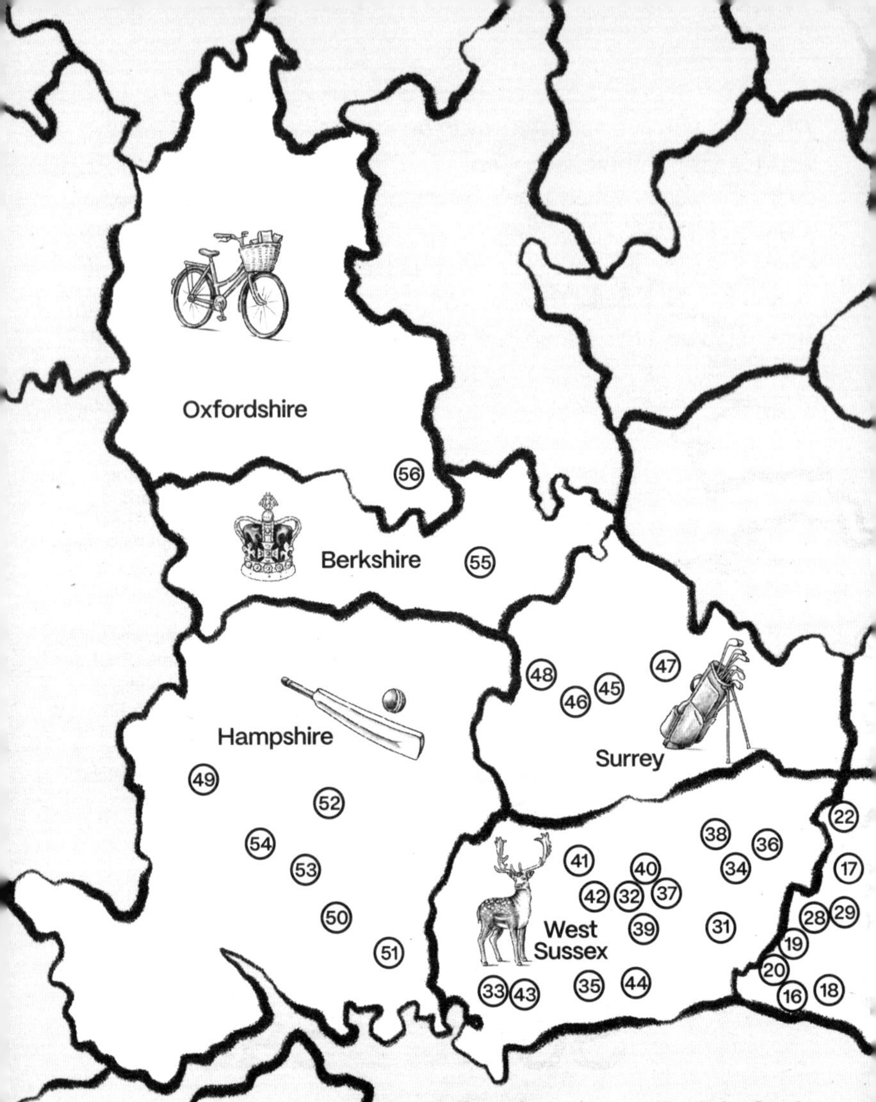

1. Balfour Winery
2. Biddenden
3. Chapel Down
4. Davenport Vineyards
5. Domaine Evremond
6. Gusbourne
7. Mereworth
8. Silverhand Estate
9. Simpsons' Wine Estate
10. Squerryes
11. The Mount Vineyard
12. Wayfarer Wines
13. Westwell
14. Woodchurch Wine Estate
15. Yotes Court
16. Artelium
17. Bluebell Vineyard Estates
18. Breaky Bottom
19. Court Garden
20. Everflyht
21. Henners
22. Kingscote Estate & Vineyard
23. Mountfield Winery
24. Mousehall
25. Oastbrook Vineyar
26. Oxney Organic Esta
27. Rathfinny

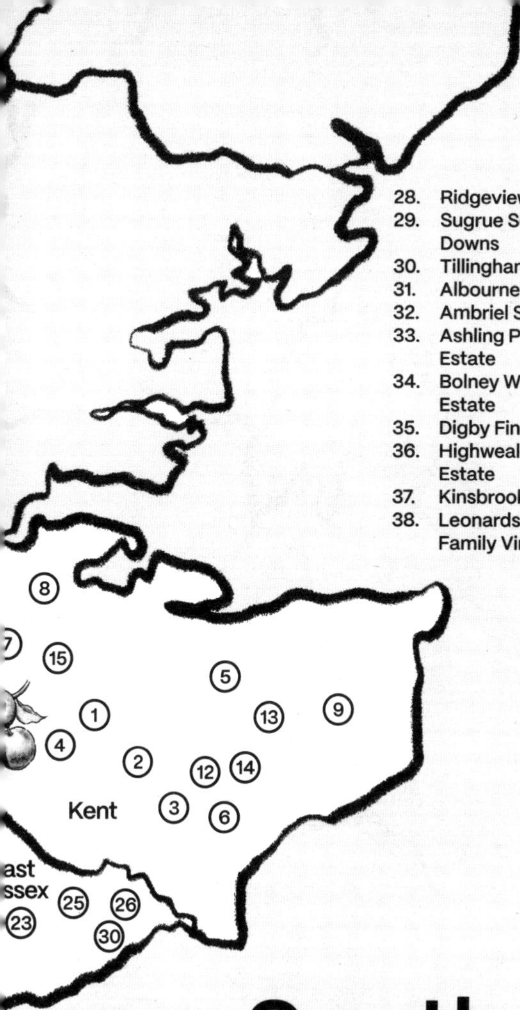

28. Ridgeview
29. Sugrue South Downs
30. Tillingham
31. Albourne Estate
32. Ambriel Sparkling
33. Ashling Park Estate
34. Bolney Wine Estate
35. Digby Fine English
36. Highweald Wine Estate
37. Kinsbrook
38. Leonardslee Family Vineyards
39. Nutbourne Vineyards
40. Nyetimber
41. Roebuck Estates
42. Stopham Estate
43. Tinwood Estate
44. Wiston Estate
45. Albury Organic Vineyard
46. Chilworth Manor
47. Denbies Wine Estate
48. Greyfriars Vineyard
49. Black Chalk
50. Exton Park Vineyard
51. Hambledon Vineyard
52. Hattingley Valley
53. Raimes English Sparkling
54. The Grange
55. Stanlake Park Wine Estate
56. Hundred Hills

South East

Responsible for producing the lion's share of wines in England, the South East offers some of my favourite wine experiences: from the Garden of England to incorporating a coastal getaway in Brighton or Rye, special memories can be made here. Boasting both the South and North Downs, the region includes a number of vineyards that are found in Outstanding Areas of Natural Beauty, and many are also located just minutes from each other – Pulborough has by far the largest concentration – making it a good base if you want to explore for longer than a day trip. Trust me, you won't ever want to leave.

Kent

Balfour Winery

An exemplary experience in the Garden of England

First and foremost, Balfour Winery is a really beautiful place to visit, situated as it is on the impressive Hush Heath Estate. My dad lives in the nearby village of Marden, which is only around five minutes away, and so I've been here a number of times, including for a girls' birthday lunch, when founder Richard Balfour-Lynn popped over to wish my friend a happy birthday! With a background in both retail and hospitality (his company previously owned Liberty department store and boutique hotel chain Hotel du Vin), it should come as no surprise that Balfour was part of the vanguard of English wine tourism, being one of the first wineries to fully embrace the idea of welcoming visitors, opening up a restaurant, shop and visitor centre (expanded greatly in 2018) to allow wine lovers to enjoy the fruits of the vine right where it is made.

And what a spot it is. It is truly stunning, with the terrace offering views of the vines, ancient woodland, orchards, wildflower meadows and even the manor. If the sun is shining, head to the expansive ground-floor decking area so that you feel as if you are almost in the vines, sipping on a chilled glass of award-winning sparkling vintage rosé, my favourite wine in the range. Indeed, when Richard and his wife Leslie planted their first five acres of vines in the Oast House Meadow in 2002, having bought Hush Heath Manor in the 1980s and then the 400-acre farm next to it, the goal was to produce an English sparkling pink to emulate their favourite Champagne, Billecart-Salmon Rosé. Happily, success swiftly followed with their inaugural vintage winning both a gold medal and a trophy at the 2007 International Wine Challenge (IWC).

There are now considerably more vineyards on the estate than those original five acres, with a variety of different grapes and clones being planted; they believe clonal selection is crucial for quality. There is Pinot Noir and Chardonnay at Old Eight Acre, rare Champagne varieties in Middle Strackney Wood – such as Arbane and Petit Meslier – and Pinot Noir, Pinot Meunier, Bacchus and Chardonnay in Nannette's Vineyard (the middle name of their daughter Jessie), to name just a few. Balfour use their own fruit and that of long-term partners with plantings in neighbouring Kent farms, in East Sussex and Essex. All vineyards are either planted on greensand (gives aromatic lift and brightness) or chalk (linearity and minerality) with the estate itself having Wealden clay soils. Winemaker Fergus Elias explains that the 'clay gives us naturally structured wines with breadth and persistence and a certain seriousness', with the diversity of all the soils allowing for complexity when blending.

The Wines

Dynamo father-and-son duo Owen and Fergus are responsible for winemaking and wine quality, and Owen has been at the winery since the very first vintage in 2004. Whilst the wines have historically been named Hush Heath, they are now all branded Balfour and the common thread is 'restraint'; they want the wines to feel composed, complete, fresh, balanced and with a quiet confidence; to be 'unapologetically English' in style.

BLANC DE BLANCS BRUT VINTAGE
toffee apple, apple crumble, honeycomb **£££££**

BRUT ROSÉ VINTAGE*
subtle cherry, cranberry, raspberry **£££££**

CINQUE PORTS (MAINLY CHARDONNAY) VINTAGE+*
spicy, apricot kernel, rounded **£££**

NANNETTE'S STILL ROSÉ VINTAGE+
watermelon, cranberry, candied fruits, dry **££**

Tours & tastings

Open daily. Choose from various options, including the Classic Tour and Tasting or the luxury Wine and Dine Experience, which includes 'hidden areas'. Enjoy a tutored tasting or simply pick up a map and follow a free, self-guided tour around the estate, finishing up with a self-guided tasting. Events throughout the year: cream teas, yoga in the vines and a premium Sunset Tour, Tasting and Dinner for something really special.

Eating

Cellar-door dining – platters and plates – is available on the ground floor, but visitors can also head upstairs to the Winemaker's Kitchen for *à la carte* dishes that showcase local and seasonal food.

Good to know

A shuttle-bus service runs from Marden station at weekends. Herbert Hall is nearby (five minutes), as is Biddenden and Chapel Down. Balfour is dog-friendly (on leads) and child-friendly in the cellar door and restaurant.

Biddenden

Kent's oldest family-owned vineyard

Biddenden might produce more juice and cider than wine, but the Barnes family first planted grapes in 1969, making them one of the oldest English grape growers and producers. Matriarch Joyce was listening to BBC's *Woman's Hour* when she heard about vineyards being planted in England, sparking a lightbulb moment. They already owned a forty-acre apple orchard but, concerned by falling prices, decided to experiment and converted a third of an acre to vines, which today totals twenty-five acres. This single estate with south-facing slopes has twelve different varieties under vine (on sandy-loam soils over clay) and has stayed true to the traditional Germanic heritage varieties typical of the time – think Reichensteiner, Acolon, Scheurebe, Schönburger and Huxelrebe, along with some Pinot Noir. Over half of the plantings are Ortega. It is still a family-run concern today, with the second and third generation now running the business. A great place to taste wines made from heritage grapes.

The Wines

Ortega is their flagship grape variety, with Germanic varieties dominating the range, allowing for a more accessible price point.

GRIBBLE BRIDGE ORTEGA DRY VINTAGE+
aromatic, tropical fruits, pear, juicy £

GERMANIC LABEL ORTEGA VINTAGE+
sweeter, pineapple cubes, mango £

GRIBBLE BRIDGE DORNFELDER VINTAGE+
fragrant, soft, red cherries, chocolate £

Tours & tastings

Self-guided tours with a tasting, guided tours, private tours and 'meet the winemaker' tours typically run from late spring until harvest.

Eating

'Nibble plate' or sharing platters of local cheese, charcuterie and chutneys are available from the slightly quirky Vineyard Shop.

Good to know

A cottage, The Grape Escape, overlooking the vines, is available to hire. Chapel Down is ten minutes away and Woodchurch and Wayfarer are nearby. Westwell and Gusbourne are around twenty-five minutes away.

Chapel Down

Superb wines in a relaxed setting

The wines at Chapel Down, found just outside the charming village of Tenterden, are unexpectedly excellent, given that this is England's largest winery, making 3 million bottles or so a year: about a third of the UK's annual production! A small, boutique producer this is not, though it once was, with English wine expert – and my dissertation mentor – Stephen Skelton MW (Master of Wine) first planting Germanic varietals at Spots Farm in 1977. He decided to sell up ten years later and the business eventually ended up being run by Frazer Thompson (he retired from this now publicly listed company in 2021 after twenty years as founder and CEO), who turned Tenterden Vineyard into Chapel Down and the English wine institution that it is today.

Grapes are sourced from their own fruit – mainly Chardonnay, Pinot Noir, Pinot Meunier and Bacchus – as well as partner vineyards that span Sussex and Essex and other vineyards in Kent too, totalling some twenty-five different sites over 1,000 acres. The most impressive, though, is Kit's Coty in the North Downs, on the Pilgrims' Way, which takes its name from a nearby Neolithic burial chamber from around 4,000 BCE, and is responsible for incredible grape quality – Kent's answer to the Crouch Valley in Essex.

All wines made at Chapel Down are not just delicious but represent good value too. From the sparkling wines (including their carbonated A Touch of Sparkle) to their popular still Bacchus, wines are distinctive and flavourful with – not surprisingly – the Kit's Coty wines really singing; every one is a top pick. Whilst supermarkets are an important route to market so, too, is wine tourism, and a lot is on offer here throughout the year, with tours and tastings running daily. Not surprisingly, this is done to scale, with a number of larger tours – a good choice for those who might feel intimidated by more intimate offerings. Expect to put on a hi-vis jacket before being taken to the Bacchus and Chardonnay vines (there is also an enchanting herb garden), and prepare to be wowed by the sheer number and size of the stainless-steel tanks, cleverly tucked away at the back of the estate.

The Wines

Winemaker Josh Donaghay-Spire is making some truly tasty wines.

BRUT NV
spice, apple crumble, nuts, lemon — ££

ROSÉ NV
red berries, red apple, citrus — ££

GRAND RESERVE VINTAGE
savoury, pecan pie, caramel — ££££

KIT'S COTY BLANC DE BLANCS VINTAGE*
elegant, lemon shortbread, croissant — £££££

KIT'S COTY COEUR DE CUVÉE VINTAGE*
hazelnuts, spice, grilled nuts, amazing — ££££££

KIT'S COTY CHARDONNAY VINTAGE+*
spice, nutmeg, apples — £££

Tours & tastings

'Informative and accessible' tours run every day, with a broad range on offer from Guided Tours and Tastings, Cheese and Wine Matching, Walkies with Wine (with dogs, summer only), wine flights and dining experiences. Self-guided vineyard walks are also available. They also host corporate events, weddings, pop-up and seasonal events, for example, Sips & Giggles comedy, yoga and theatre in the vines. The Wine Sanctuary tasting room (for up to sixty people) is available for private events.

Eating

The Swan is an independent restaurant from the I'll Be Mother group, sourcing local ingredients with a private dining room and a chef's table. There's a small selection of food at the cellar-door shop, including cheese and charcuterie boards and sandwiches. BYO picnic. Horsebox pop-up bar outside in high season.

Good to know

Over ten tours a day run in the summer. Children are allowed, but there is a charge. Dogs allowed on site and in the cellar door but not at the restaurant or on the tours. Biddenden, Woodchurch and Wayfarer Wines are all around ten minutes away with Balfour being thirty.

Davenport Vineyards

Will Davenport's love of wine took him all over the world, from Alsace to California and even Roseworthy College, South Australia before returning to England and working at a winery in Hampshire. He planted his first five acres of vines in 1991 in Horsmonden and what began as a hobby – he initially planned to just sell the grapes – instead became England's first organic vineyard. When the winery he'd been working for folded, he bought their equipment and a farm in nearby Rotherfield, East Sussex, and has been quietly but passionately and humbly making his wines ever since.

Right from the start, he was determined to make them organic, despite rot being an issue in our wet climate, and so learnt about *Botrytis* (a type of fungus) control, getting the vines in balance, canopy management, and working with the soil to make it healthy. His five acres grew to twenty-four and they were certified by the Soil Association in 2020, with plantings including Chardonnay, Pinot Noir, Pinot Meunier, Ortega, Bacchus and Huxelrebe. He also practises minimal intervention in the winery with no added yeast, and minimal sulphur and filtration.

Historically, there has been no visitor offering or experience at Davenport, but a (rather lovely) cellar-door shop has recently opened. There is also a balcony and terrace with views across to the orchards and, excitingly, tastings are in the pipeline, so watch this space as this iconic estate opens up to thirsty guests!

Domaine Evremond

The elegant Anglo-French alliance with Champagne Taittinger

This new addition to the English wine scene opened to the public in the spring of 2025 and encapsulates good taste and understated luxury. Patrick McGrath MW, the charming chairman and founder of wine agency Hatch Mansfield, was keen to add an English winery to his portfolio, and whilst discussing his plans with friend Pierre-Emmanuel Taittinger (president of Champagne Taittinger), whose wines he imports, it was decided that they would make their own wine instead.

Both the non-vintage Classic Cuvée and winery are named after Charles de Saint-Évremond (1613–1703). Charles was a French aristocrat who popularised the wines of Champagne at the court of Charles II, and with whom the Taittinger family have had a long-held fascination. Not only is the wine named after him, but the estate's emblem or motif is also inspired by Évremond: the cinquefoil – a five-petalled flower – which was his crest. He's also the only Frenchman to be buried at Poet's Corner in Westminster Abbey, making his name a perfect fit for this vinous marriage, bringing French elegance to the Kent countryside. In an Area of Outstanding Natural Beauty 152 acres of vines were planted in 2017 on south-facing chalky land that had previously been home predominantly to apple and pear orchards – all overseen by the Taittinger team. Once planting was underway, a winery needed building, and the winery, cellar door and tasting room are simply breathtaking, melding sympathetically with the environment. The largely subterranean winery is comprised of two storeys: B2, which is the underground working cellar, and B1, which is the press hall and tank room – visible through windows from the spacious tasting room. Wildflower meadows, orchards and vines surround the picturesque plot, with a large table made by designer Sebastian Cox – from one long piece of Lebanon cedar – taking pride of place outside, for visitors to sit around.

The Wines

The grapes might be English, but they are grown by French viticulturalist Christelle Rinville and made by winemaker Alexandre Ponnavoy from a blend of the classic three varieties (currently Pinot Noir-dominant, although, ultimately, Chardonnay will take centre stage), with three years spent on the yeast lees.

CLASSIC CUVÉE EDITION I NV
golden apples, nuts, honeysuckle **£££££**

CLASSIC CUVÉE EDITION II NV
tarte tatin, pecans, complex, layered **£££££**

Tours & tastings

The cellar door is open all year round; check the website for specific days. There is a Classic Cuvée tasting or a more in-depth Domaine Tour.

Eating

A monthly (weekends only) premium food and fizz experience, the Flavours of Kent, celebrates seasonal food. There are also relaxed brunch pop-ups with oysters and seafood; no need to book.

Good to know

Drop-ins are welcome and guests can enjoy a glass (or two) of Classic Cuvée on the (dog-friendly) terrace – weather allowing. It can get breezy, so take a jumper. Canterbury is a short drive away and Chartham Vineyard just under ten minutes.

Gusbourne

One of England's most appealing and awarded estates

Who would have thought that what was once a deeply forgettable swathe of arable land – or turnip fields – would one day be responsible for producing some of the most acclaimed wines in the country? But South African Andrew Weeber couldn't help but notice how mild the weather was in Appledore when he visited his daughter at home there, and in 2003 purchased the site with the sole purpose of producing premium sparkling wines.

The name chosen for the venture was Gusbourne, named after the original landowner, John de Goosebourne, who founded the estate in 1410, with his crest – showing three geese – still visible in Appledore Church. Indeed, these geese very much inspire the logo and label today, with a goose found on the label, another on the top of the foil and a third on the muzzle (the wire cage) cap.

The first vines were planted here the following year (2004), with predominantly Burgundian clones of Chardonnay, Pinot Noir and Pinot Meunier being used, which give lower yields but greater complexity. The balance were Champagne clones. Unusually, the soils weren't chalk, but Wealden clay over sand, which retains heat and gives more character to the wines. There is also a maritime influence, with the vines being about six miles from the coast: Rye, Camber Sands and Dungeness can all be seen from the estate on a clear day, looking out over the gentle south-facing slopes to Romney Marsh and the sea beyond; this land used to be under water.

There are now almost 140 acres planted at Appledore, with a further seventy acres in West Sussex. These vines are planted on chalk and contribute freshness and minerality to the blends, alongside the richer wines from grapes grown on clay. Sustainable practices are adhered to – they are SWGB Gold certified – and they take care to be as respectful to the land as possible.

Wines produced here are stellar, with around 95 per cent being sparkling. A still Chardonnay, rosé and Pinot Noir are also made – with the latter in particular selling out very quickly – but fizz is the focus at their on-site winery, with small amounts (around 5–15 per cent) of oak being used on the base blends to add weight, texture and mouthfeel; they want their wines to be complex, with some richness. Unusually, an exemplary sweet Chardonnay is also made.

Feeling that the best place to showcase their wines is at the estate, Gusbourne opened the Nest in 2017, which offers a premium experience. Downstairs is the cellar-door shop with barrel tables and stools, whilst upstairs is the tasting room and dining area for tour lunches. Outside, a covered garden terrace allows for al fresco vineyard platters, with views over the estate, with further pop-up spaces opening up over the summer to allow guests to make the most of this truly unique place; one I very highly recommend.

The Wines

Only vintage wines are made from their own fruit, and since 2023 by Mary Bridges.

BRUT RESERVE VINTAGE*
spice, apple crumble, broad, excellent **££££**

BLANC DE BLANCS VINTAGE*
elegant, peanut brittle, croissant **£££££**

ROSÉ VINTAGE
cherry blossom, raspberry pip, clementine **£££££**

CHARDONNAY GUINEVERE VINTAGE+*
apricot, spice, banana **£££**

Tours & tastings
Cellar door open daily. Sparkling Tasting Flight (self-guided), Limited Edition Wines Tasting Flight, Estate Tour with Lunch (monthly changing menu), Classic Vineyard Tour & Tasting, Icons Experience with Lunch. Self-guided walking tour with map: dogs allowed on leads. Masterclasses, seasonal and special events. Private and corporate events: Winemaker's Library, a private dining space. Gusbourne membership.

Eating
Vineyard Platters for Two. A three-course meal as part of the Estate Tour with Lunch. Chef Series.

Good to know
Highly awarded: a Walpole British Luxury Brand of the Year, previously ranked #28 in the World's Best Vineyards and #29 in Forbes' Top 50 Wineries. Part of the 163-mile Saxon Shore Way (a footpath) passes through the property.

Mereworth

A characterful, rustic-chic winery and tap room

This family-owned site where the winery and tap room is located was gifted to Will Boscawen by his grandfather, along with a farm and some land. Once a hop-processing plant called Brewers' Hall Oast – George Orwell once picked hops here, until he got tuberculosis and ended up in Maidstone Hospital – it had been mothballed since 1989.

On returning from working abroad, Will moved to the farm in Kent and spoke to the East Malling Research Station (since the 2016 takeover also known as NIAB: the National Institute of Agricultural Botany, focused on innovation and research), who confirmed that the land would be more than suitable for vines.

The vineyards themselves are found in nearby Wateringbury (a very cute village, where I got married!) on a south-facing, gently sloping, greensand ridge; loamy soil with a subsoil of ragstone. Now totalling around 7.5 acres, they were first planted in 2015 to Chardonnay, Pinot Noir and Pinot Meunier.

Winemaker Scott Gebbie made the first vintage in 2018, releasing the wines during lockdown. Only single-vintage sparkling wines are made, as well as Marourde, a mead. Nearly all the wines are sold on site, which boasts an open-plan, wooden, Scandi-vibe café, bar, tasting room and tap room.

The Wines

Mereworth makes delicious sparkling wines.

WHITE FROM WHITE VINTAGE
expressive, honey, honeysuckle, marzipan £££££

WHITE FROM BLACK VINTAGE
toasty, nuts, savoury, berry fruits £££££

PINK VINTAGE
rosehip, raspberry, cherry cobbler £££££

Tours & tastings
Small-group tours and tasting or a self-guided wine flight. Private tours on request. Available for private hire. Also weekend jazz brunch and seasonal markets.

Eating
The Counter serves hot and cold food with brunch, pizza and a sparkling afternoon tea (must be pre-booked) available at the weekends.

Good to know
Yotes Court is a five-minute drive away with Balfour, Silverhand, Squerryes, Wildwood Vineyard, Birchden Vineyards and The Mount all around thirty minutes in the car.

Silverhand Estate

The organic estate championing Charmat method fizz

A rather bumpy drive down a rustic, rural track eventually brings you to Silverhand Estate, named after the fictional King Ludd, who lost his hand in battle in the first century and had a silver hand made for him. It is now the largest single organic vineyard in the UK (it was an organic vegetable farm before), spanning over 900 acres on Kimmeridgian clay and chalk soils.

The first 500 acres of vines were planted in spring 2019, initially to Chardonnay, Pinot Noir, Pinot Meunier, Solaris and Bacchus, but now there are sixteen varieties, including experimental ones (for England), such as Colombard and Gamay. Five years after planting, work started on a cosy cellar door, converting a barn that was already there. In the same year, Silverhand was the first vineyard in the UK to reach carbon-negative status; they even have their own conservation team.

Their flagship wines – Silver Reign Brut and Rosé Brut NV – are made by the Charmat, or tank method. This is the same way that Prosecco is produced and allows for a more accessible price point. It does, however, give the wines quite a different taste profile to the traditional method sparklings that are typically made in England; they are lighter and more fruit-forward, ideal for those who prefer easy-drinking fizz. They are also behind the (somewhat offensively named) Harlot range, with plans to take total production to over 4 million bottles, surpassing even Chapel Down.

The Wines

Both Charmat and traditional method sparkling wines are made by winemaker Theo Cullen.

SILVER REIGN BRUT NV
light, pear, apple blossom £

CLASSIC BRUT NV
honeysuckle, apricot cobbler, oats ££

SOLARIS VINTAGE+
nectarine, apricot, grapefruit £

Tours & tastings
Self-guided wine flights, guided tastings, vineyard and winery tours, vineyard safari, walking tour, picnic in the vines, summer sunset tour, history tours, sip and paint, weekend late-night openings, private tours available.

Eating
The Lion pub – like the estate, it is also owned by MDCV UK – is next to the cellar door.

Good to know
Yotes Court, Mereworth and The Mount aren't too far away.

Simpsons' Wine Estate

Bringing French savoir-faire to Kent

Winemakers Charles and Ruth Simpson have been working at Domaine Sainte Rose in the Hérault, Languedoc since they bought it in 2002, and after living there for ten years decided to return to England. Excited by the opportunities here – especially with regards to sparkling wine – they established Simpsons' and now divide their time between the two wineries.

The vineyards are all found around the extremely picturesque village of Barham, with its green-spired church, and wines are made only from their own fruit, grown across ninety-four acres and three vineyards: Roman Road, Railway Hill and Bonny Bush Hill. The first vines of Chardonnay, Pinot Noir and Pinot Meunier were planted in 2014 (at Roman Road) on the chalk soils of the Elham Valley of the North Downs, with around twenty-five different clones, mainly Champagne and Burgundy, being used. Sustainability is taken seriously here: improving the health of the soil, composting, using sheep in the vineyards, animal manure, cover crops and seaweed sprays. They are even experimenting with PIWIs.

A barn from the original pig farm was converted into a winery in 2016 and above that is the Glass House Tasting Room; a beautiful space for trying the wines. Whilst the intention originally was to focus on sparkling wines, after the high-quality 2018 vintage they started making still wines, and now more of these are being made than sparkling; do try their Railway Hill rosé. Demand for tours and tastings are growing as consumers look for immersive experiences that also tap into the trend for eating and drinking seasonally, locally and sustainably, and a fun way to finish your visit is by going down the helter-skelter slide into the winery before chuckling at the excellent unisex loo signs!

The Wines

All wines are vegan and a mix of still and sparkling.

CHALKLANDS CLASSIC CUVÉE NV
apple blossom, nuts, marzipan — £££

CANTERBURY ROSE SPARKLING ROSÉ VINTAGE
summer berries, strawberry, savoury — £££

FLINT FIELDS BLANC DE NOIRS VINTAGE*
cherry, spice, blueberry — ££££

RAILWAY HILL ROSÉ VINTAGE+*
pretty pink, strawberry, berries, flavourful — ££

THE ROMAN ROAD CHARDONNAY VINTAGE+*
oak, butterscotch, apricot, oatmeal — £££

Tours & tastings

Informative but intimate, with a weekly Wine Tasting Experience running all year round (sometimes twice a week) in the afternoons. There is also a Tour and Tasting Experience twice a month. Sunset sessions on some evenings in the summer. Pop-up events like Sip and Snip (flower arranging with a wine tasting). Private and corporate events.

Eating

Ad hoc offerings such as Mother's Day tea and exclusive dining events.

Good to know

Only twenty minutes from Domaine Evremond and thirty from Westwell.

Squerryes

Beating the Champenois at their own game!

It wasn't until Champagne house Duval-Leroy came sniffing around Squerryes (pronounced 'sq-air-reys') that the idea of starting a wine business even occurred to Henry Warde. The estate (farming, mainly – arable and dairy) had been in the family since 1731, with him being the eighth generation, but this fortuitous French visit fostered the idea to put vines in themselves, which they duly did. In 2006 they planted fifty-three acres (of the 2,500-acre estate) with Chardonnay, Pinot Noir and Pinot Meunier on the chalk-rich soils of the North Downs, on the Pilgrims' Way, in order to make traditional method sparkling wines. Their first vintage was in 2010, with Henry's father John describing those four years as 'the long, thirsty wait'.

Historically, wines were made at Henners, a producer further south, but a new winery opened on site in 2024, with ex-Gusbourne winemaker Tom Barratt-Jones at the helm. The Brut Vintage is a blend of the three classic varietals, and the Rosé is 80 per cent Pinot Noir. Both wines go through MLF, with three years on lees; the Blanc de Blancs has around five.

Opening the site up to visitors has been an organic process of growth, starting with the first-floor restaurant (somewhat reminiscent of a golf club) in 2017, which has proved immensely successful, as has a membership scheme inspired by a trip to California: members can commit to twelve bottles annually, and receive discounts and invitations to events such as the annual summer garden party. In front of the main garden terrace is a showpiece vineyard – the Rosé Vineyard – and a sprawling lawn. As their motto, *Licet esse beatis* states, 'It is permitted to be joyful', and spending time here sipping these sublime sparkling wines is most certainly that.

The Wines

Only vintage sparkling wines are made.

BRUT VINTAGE
elegant, lemon curd, nutty £££££

BLANC DE BLANCS VINTAGE*
fresh, almond croissant, praline £££££

ROSÉ VINTAGE
rose petals, red berries, macaron £££££

Tours & tastings

Tasting flights available in the Tasting Bar or book in for a tasting experience or a tasting experience and lunch. Tours and tastings run from late spring until end of October. Member events. Private hire. Bespoke experiences.

Eating

The two-AA Rosette Winery Restaurant is open all year round for lunch, with dinner served at the weekend. The Vineyard Café opens in the spring. Afternoon tea is served in the Tasting Bar. Sunday roasts. Deli and cellar door.

Good to know

The Mount Vineyard is around twenty minutes away and Westerham Brewery is next door. For *Bridgerton* fans, Squerryes Court featured in season three.

The Mount Vineyard

Eat, drink and make merry at this welcoming locale

On reflection, I'm not entirely sure how I failed to notice that this entire enterprise is essentially in the Greenwoods' back garden! A rather tight driveway (very easy to miss) takes you down to the parking area, gift shop and tennis court before having to walk past the rather grand family house to visit the restaurant or vineyards. It was finding this dream house in 2011 that prompted Simon Greenwood and his wife Sarah to move out of London, and it just so happened to come with a vineyard. One that had been planted in 2004, in this picturesque part of the Darenth Valley, with Bacchus, Phoenix, Pinot Noir, Regent, Rondo, Seyval Blanc and Siegerrebe. They decided to keep it on, and even added two further acres of Chardonnay, taking the total acreage to ten.

Knowing that their wines needed a route to market, they decided to sell them on site and, five years later, after careful planning, they started welcoming visitors. There is an inviting conservatory-style restaurant (the stone-baked pizzas are popular) and an outside wooden wine deck (favoured by dog walkers and larger groups). In the summer the Flint Bar and tipi opens next to the verdant vines, with benches to sit on by the stretch tent to soak up the view.

The wine range is fairly concise; there are a handful of core wines (though the still rosé sells out extremely fast) with the approach in the winery being one of restraint and refinement, focusing on purity of fruit, balance and elegance. Their sparkling white is Chardonnay-dominant, with some Seyval Blanc and Phoenix, and the sparkling rosé utilises the same grapes, with the addition of Pinot Noir, whilst the juicy Cellar Key Red is a blend of Rondo and Regent.

The Wines

Made by Litmus Wines.

SPARKLING ROSÉ VINTAGE
peach, redcurrant, grapefruit, rosehip **££££**

FLINT KEY BACCHUS VINTAGE+
fresh, citrus, grapefruit, lemon verbena **££**

CELLAR KEY VINTAGE+
deep colour, cherries, plums, dark chocolate **££**

Tours & tastings

Tastings at weekends; in the Wine Loft during the winter and in the Oak Terrace during the summer. Tours only take place in peak season in the summer months. There is also an impressive calendar of events, such as lino printing, comedy nights, flowerpot painting and an end-of-season summer festival. Private and corporate events, as well as weddings, can be held here.

Eating

The Courtyard Restaurant and Bar is a buzzy, bistro-style restaurant with a retractable roof and bifold doors that is open all year round. Summer BBQs at the Flint Bar. Tempting Ten Acres gift shop and cellar door.

Good to know

The Greenwoods also own the gorgeous olde-worlde gastropub – the Samuel Palmer – across the road, which has three beautifully appointed bedrooms.

Wayfarer Wines

It is genuinely joyful, that thrill of discovery when stumbling across a new vineyard, which is quite honestly how I came across Wayfarer which, rather charmingly, means pilgrim, whilst exploring other local wineries. There are seven tasty still wines to try, made at contractor Defined Wine, from grapes grown on the Ashford family's two vineyards. First planted in 2016, they currently total around eight acres, with plans to double this. I highly recommend the Pilgrims' Way Pinot Gris vintage, Steve's Blend Bacchus/Ortega vintage and Woodland Chardonnay vintage.

Tours are weekends only, from a self-guided vineyard tour and tasting to a guided one. Cheese and charcuterie can be added on. A cellar door (selling covetable upcycled wine-bottle candles) and shop opened in 2021. Woodchurch is only three minutes away.

Westwell

A funky, low-intervention winery

Westwell pretty much encapsulates all that is captivating about the 'new wave' of wineries that can now be found around England, along with the likes of Gutter & Stars, Langham, Saddle Goose and Sandridge Barton. Forgoing the comparatively well-trodden path of making traditional method sparklers conventionally, many are striking out in a new direction, and the results are electric and exciting. From making skin-contact and Pét-Nat wines to using wild ferment and amphoras, the wines are experimental, with an emphasis on being sustainable and respecting the land via regenerative farming. As winemaker and managing director Adrian Pike says, you need to 'plant well, respect the soil and make great, honest wines from brilliant fruit'.

This fruit – at the heart of everything that they do – comes from thirty-six acres under vine (owned by the Taylor family) in Kent and plantings include five different varieties: Ortega, Chardonnay, Pinot Noir, Pinot Meunier and a smattering of Regent. Adrian oversees the processing of this fruit at the winery, which is just beneath the Pilgrims' Way, an ancient route historically used by pilgrims walking to the shrine of St Thomas Becket, on the North Downs. Not always a winemaker, before working at Westwell Adrian was in the music industry, whilst wife Galia was in the band Psapp, who wrote the theme tune for *Grey's Anatomy*. But a chance encounter with a bottle of English organic wine in Soho, made by Will Davenport, saw a fairly immediate change in career path. So captivated was he by this wine that he called Will the next day and started working for him whilst starting his wine studies, eventually taking over at Westwell in 2017.

Adrian and Galia's striking but sympathetic aesthetic is stamped all over the winery – think warm wood and string lighting – with visitors extremely welcome: 'Hospitality and community are at the heart of what we do.'

The Wines

Adrian oversees winemaking, whilst Galia is responsible for the arresting labels that adorn all the bottles, giving the brand a really strong visual identity – they look incredible all lined up on the shelf.

PELEGRIM NV*
buttered toast, broad, honeycomb, excellent **£££**

(UN)NATURALLY PETULANT PINK VINTAGE*
cherry, raspberry, red apple **££**

ORTEGA VINTAGE+
orchard fruits, hedgerow, peach skin **£**

Tours & tastings
Tours and tastings run throughout the year over the weekends, or tread out into the vineyard using a QR code for a self-guided audio tour and order a Westwell picnic to go with you. Masterclasses, yoga, Walk + Wine, lino cutting, screen printing, supper clubs, theatre in the vines and even an annual dog show!

Eating
Local charcuterie and cheese plates as well as toasties. Pizza Fridays run throughout the spring and summer months (as do weekend food trucks).

Good to know
Westwell provide the raw materials for the Pelegrims skincare range. Dogs and children are welcome.

Woodchurch Wine Estate

First-class fizz alongside sweeping vineyard views

The sparkling wines here are absolutely stellar, with the Classic NV and Chardonnay Brut Vintage being two of my top discoveries of the entire research trip. Graham and Donna Barbour, who established this picturesque, single-estate, vineyard – planted with over twelve acres of different clones of Chardonnay, Pinot Noir, Pinot Meunier and Bacchus in 2010 – wanted to produce both still and sparkling wines but it is the latter that really shine. The first vintage was released in 2015 with fêted winemaker Dermot Sugrue originally making the sparkling wines, before setting up Sugrue South Downs in 2022.

Still wines (a Field white blend, a rosé and sometimes a Chardonnay) are made by Matthieu Elzinga at Litmus Wines, who has also taken over making the sparkling range, and the approach in the winery mirrors that of the vineyard: minimal intervention with a focus on fruit-forward wine style that expresses the character of the site and vintage.

Open all year round, this is a really delightful spot with the outdoor tables and balcony overlooking the vines, and sweeping views out to Romney Marsh and Dungeness, sharing the same outlook as nearby Gusbourne. The interior décor is stylish, with a tasting space and cellar door on the ground floor and the restaurant upstairs. A striking pheasant logo – designed by Donna as a nod to all the game birds found in the vineyard – graces a wall of this extremely charming space. Four friends, Kelly, John, Donna (a different Donna!) and Darren, have recently taken over ownership.

The Wines

Both still and sparkling wines are made, with the fizz being excellent.

Wine	Price
CLASSIC BRUT NV* delicious, nutty, spice, toast	£££
CHARDONNAY BRUT VINTAGE* distinctive, honeycomb, pecans, toffee apple	££££
ROSÉ BRUT VINTAGE raspberry, pink grapefruit, appealing	£££

Tours & tastings

Free self-guided vineyard walk (with map), wine flight with tasting notes, guided tour and tasting. Visit with wine tours such as Shuttle & Vine or English Wine Tasting Tours. Wedding receptions.

Eating

The restaurant serves snacks, small plates, cheese and charcuterie boards, and there is a pizza oven on weekends in high season.

Good to know

Wayfarer is down the road, Gusbourne is ten minutes away, and both Chapel Down and Biddenden are close. Dog-friendly outside.

Yotes Court

Picnic on the Paddock Lawn with vine views

Yotes Court, along with its beautiful gardens, orchard and soft-fruit farm, was bought by Susannah and her husband Rich Ricci (not to be confused with fictional movie character Richie Rich!) in 2008, but it wasn't until 2016 that they planted fifty acres of Chardonnay, Pinot Noir and Pinot Meunier, initially selling their fruit to Chapel Down. Today, a further seventy-five acres of south-facing slopes with greensand and ragstone soils are under vine, with the stones acting like a suntrap at the base of the vines, much like the *galets* (large 'pudding' stones) in Châteauneuf-du-Pape.

They are keen advocates of sustainability and regenerative agriculture, and their viticulturalist, Tony Purdie, helped establish the Sustainable Wines of Great Britain initiative, of which they were a founding member, now holding the Gold Standard. Practically, this means using special sprays (such as seaweed, which improves vine health), sheep for mowing and pheromone moth traps. They also work with the East Malling Research Station on PIWIs, including Divico, a Swiss cross of Gamaret and Bronner which buds late, so is naturally resistant to frost, and ripens early. Yotes Court was the first producer to use this 'Kent Claret' from the 2021 vintage, making ninety bottles, which they doubled in 2022.

Wines are predominantly still – there are a few sparkling ones – with the labels reflecting the Riccis' other passion: horses. They are the proud owners of around forty racehorses, with their grey mare, Lossiemouth, winning at Cheltenham one year. As such, wine names are rather fun, and include 'Starter's Orders', 'Best Turned Out' and 'Loose Rein'. Next to the Paddock Lawn, by the picnic tables – which offer expansive views across the vines and beyond from this slightly elevated position – is a striking pink horse feature with green spots. Giddy up!

The Wines

Made at contractor Defined Wine, with all names being horse-related.

LIVELOVELAUGH PINOT GRIS SPARKLING VINTAGE
lemon sherbet, orchard fruits, blossom **£££**

BEST TURNED OUT ROSÉ VINTAGE+
red berries, raspberry, pomegranate **££**

STARTER'S ORDERS PINOT NOIR VINTAGE+
lifted, plums, spice, raspberry **££**

Tours & tastings

From spring until harvest. Self-guided wine flights and a pick and mix of vineyard tour, flight, guided tasting and lunch. Can visit as part of Wine Tours of Kent.

Eating

Cheese and charcuterie boards on the Paddock Lawn or at the cellar-door barn. Or bring your own picnic. Off-season afternoon tea in the tasting room.

Good to know

Mereworth is very close, The Mount about thirty minutes away. Children and dogs welcome.

East Sussex

Artelium

Practically perfect in every way!

When visiting Artelium – which celebrates the union of wine, nature and art – be sure to look for the memorable giant V on the nearby slopes of the South Downs. Over 3,000 trees were planted in 1897 to commemorate the Golden Jubilee of Queen Victoria and can easily be seen from the vineyard, which was planted by Julie Bretland and husband Mark Collins in 2018. A long-held interest in wine, which saw them serving English wines at their 2013 wedding, eventually culminated in the creation of their own vineyards and winery.

There are two separate sites and both have vineyards: one in Streat, East Sussex, where the cellar door is, with the other, larger site found in Madehurst, West Sussex, where, in 2021, vineyards were planted and the winery built, ready for their first vintage the following year. Streat has around twenty acres of clay and Madehurst forty-five acres of chalk, with varieties such as Chardonnay, Pinot Noir, Pinot Meunier and Pinot Gris; Champagne, Burgundy and Alsace clones are used. Artelium also have an impressive amount of PIWI plantings, reflecting the couple's obvious commitment to sustainability, such as Souvignier Gris, Sauvignac and Voltis for whites and Pinotin, Divico and Cabaret Noir for reds. Around 10 per cent of their plantings are now PIWIs.

Consultant winemaker Owen Elias, South African winemaker Solly Monyamane and Mark make the still and sparkling wines, with the limited release Artefact range being a highlight. The (sadly sold out) Cabaret Noir – a PIWI grape – is soooo good, as is the Pinot Gris (below), whilst the Artefact Prize offers an artist the chance to collaborate on the labels. Art clearly runs through the veins of the entire estate (no surprise, given its name), with sculptures dotting the grounds, including one by Rosie Mortimer, a previous winner of the prize, whose work now graces a couple of striking labels.

Unsurprisingly, there is a creative aesthetic here (even the ceramic spittoons are gorgeous), yet it is warm and approachable; like many wineries, this used to be a farm, so many of the converted buildings are cosy and characterful. A terrace by the vines is a splendid summer spot, and the tasting room and cellar door are inviting all year round. Happily, this is one of my closest wineries!

The Wines

The core range sparklers are superlative.

CURATORS CUVÉE VINTAGE*
citrus, nuts, apple strudel, lemon meringue **£££**

MAKERS ROSÉ VINTAGE
raspberry clafoutis, almond, redcurrant **££££**

ARTEFACT #11 MAIDEN HARVEST PINOT GRIS+*
textured, spicy, pear, delicious **£££**

Tours & tastings
Drop-in tastings, public tours from April to end of September, and a raft of creative events throughout the year, from workshops to exhibitions and markets.

Eating
Offering local, seasonal food with feasting menus served 'family style'. Sunday roasts. Supper clubs. BBQs.

Good to know
Keen equestrians can arrive by horse and use the stables.

Bluebell Vineyard Estates

Owner Barry Tay and his wife Joyce (who has since sadly passed away) first planted Chardonnay, Pinot Noir and Pinot Meunier vines over twenty years ago, although the number of plantings has now grown to around ten different varieties. Wines are made under two distinct labels – Hindleap for their sparkling wines and Ashdown for their still. Sparklings include a one-of-a-kind Merlot, both a single varietal Pinot Meunier and Seyval Blanc, along with a classic cuvée, a rosé and two Blanc de Blancs, one of which is barrel-aged. The Ashdown wines boast a single varietal Chardonnay, Merlot, Ortega and even a Chasselas (a Swiss grape). Tours and tastings run on certain days of the week, but there are also self-guided tastings. Or simply enjoy a vineyard walk, best enjoyed in bluebell season (mid-spring) when they carpet the woodland behind.

Breaky Bottom

No book on English wine would be complete without including the legendary Peter Hall from Breaky Bottom, who died in October 2025. I met him whilst researching my Master of Wine dissertation, and he encapsulated the true passion and grit of the pioneering English winemakers, first planting Seyval Blanc – from which he made many of his iconic sparkling wines – in 1974. Breaky Bottom continues to sell wine from the cellar door; by appointment only.

Court Garden

A self-described 'chirpy chap' winemaker and second-generation owner Hugo Corney simply radiates enthusiasm and passion for this wonderful, single-estate vineyard. His parents Howard and Jenny first planted vines at Court Gardens Farm – which sits on land originally owned by Anne of Cleves – in 2005 (diversifying from breeding ewes) and there are now ten varieties planted: Chardonnay, Pinot Noir, Pinot Meunier, Pinot Noir Précoce, Rondo, Ortega, Pinot Blanc, Pinot Gris, Arbane and Petit Meslier which make eight different, delicious, good value wines and two vermouths. Tours and tastings are available throughout the year by appointment and are hosted by either Hugo or Howard with a picnic lunch made by Jenny. If you want to experience the warmth and sense of place of a small, family-run winery then don't hesitate to come here; it's a true gem.

Everflyht

Located just outside the village of Ditchling – six minutes from Court Garden – Everflyht, which is owned by Ben and Sam Ellis, have recently embraced hospitality, offering seasonal weekend tours and tastings with private and corporate events during the week. Tours are run by General Manager and viticulturalist Luke Spalding who keenly follows regenerative principles in the vineyard, including an organic spray programme, cover crops and rotations. The new tasting room is gorgeous and their top-notch range of wines – sparkling only which are made at Hambledon – can be enjoyed here or outside next to the vines. Food includes cheeseboards, charcuterie, bread and salads. A stunning spot.

Henners

Visit for delicious, joyful drinking

Larry Warr, an ex-Formula One engineer, first planted vines at Henners – named after his marvellously monikered French ancestor Henners Dubois (who fled to England during the French Revolution) – in 2007, putting in multiple clones of the classic three Champagne varieties on seven acres of free-draining clay soils mixed with sand. The land is gently sloping, with a low elevation and, being only five miles from the coast, benefits from sea breezes, which add a certain salinity to the wines, as well as mitigating against disease and frost pressure; free-flowing air is hugely beneficial in protecting vines from both.

Larry started selling his wines in 2012 through UK agency and distributor Boutinot, and ten years after the vines first went in, they jumped at the chance to buy the business. Wines are now made by Collette O'Leary, who took over the reins in 2019, from a mix of estate and partner fruit, making styles that are intended to be fun, elegant, well-made, moreish and joyful; wines that people want to drink and take home. But they are also well crafted and considered, using reserve wines, oak for depth and richness and different clonal parcels for layers of complexity.

Like many an English winery, Henners is becoming more outward facing and increasingly keen to welcome visitors, who they say will 'have a lovely time and feel really looked after'. The cellar door and tasting room were built in 2022 in order to be able to do just this, and offer tours and tastings, which started the same year and are constantly evolving.

Wines are the same price to drink on site as to take away, and they have an 'open house', relaxed vibe, with friendly, welcoming staff.

The Wines

Excellent vintage fizz and fruity, moreish still wines – the Pinot Noir is a fave.

BRUT NV
lightly floral, marzipan, elegant **££££**

BRUT VINTAGE
brioche, croissant, citrus **££££**

PINOT NOIR ROSÉ VINTAGE+*
crunchy red fruits, fresh, poised **££**

PINOT NOIR VINTAGE+*
fun, fruity, soft, charming **££**

Tours & tastings

Tours and tastings run all year round (weekends only): cheese and wine tastings in the winter and tours commencing in the spring. Cheese or charcuterie boards can be added on. They also host a spring and summer party and the Big Christmas Wine Tasting. Seasonal events, monthly quiz nights, horsebox summer bar. Cellar door.

Eating

Regular pop-up food partnerships (pizza, Mexican, Nepalese), as well as tasting platters.

Good to know

Dog-friendly, family-friendly, hen-do-friendly. Nearby is Hidden Spring Vineyard and the Secret Vineyard (at Lime Cross Nursery), where you can stay in an ÖÖD house (a mirrored glass cabin) or a shepherd's hut. They even make their own wine.

Kingscote Estate & Vineyard

Kingscote has changed hands a few times over the last fifteen years, with founder Christian Monge – who first planted vines here in 2010 – sadly passing away in 2016. The estate was then bought by Mark Dixon's MDCV UK, who now owns Silverhand Estate, but is currently owned by the Nair family, who bought the manor house, along with its seventy acres of organic vines. Tours and tastings run at the weekends, and the cellar door (the original tithe barn) is open seven days a week. Hot food is served from the kitchen. Afternoon teas. Event space. Child-friendly. Private tours. Coach House cottage to rent.

Mountfield Winery

The extremely picturesque Mountfield Court has been in the same family for generations but in 2012 Lucinda and Simon Fraser decided to plant vines – Chardonnay, Pinot Noir and Pinot Meunier – and now make a small range of three superb sparkling wines, made by talented winemaker Ulrich Hoffmann of Hoffmann and Rathbone fame. Stables were converted into a tasting room – open during the summer months at the weekend – and an old dairy became the winery.

Mousehall

Delightful boutique winery and distillery

This historic, quintessentially English property – like Nyetimber, it is mentioned in the Domesday Book – is the second wine venture and home from home of the South African Jordan family, responsible for such iconic wines as 'Nine Yards' Chardonnay. Gary and Kathy were keen to turn their hands to Northern Hemisphere winemaking too, and England seemed the logical place to do this, so the search for somewhere suitable started.

After about a year they found Mousehall, named after former owner James de Mouleshale or James of Mousehall, and saw both the beauty and the potential of the site. Lying within the High Weald Area of Outstanding Natural Beauty, the estate is tiny – totalling only two acres – but despite there being just a field with poor drainage and lots of trees where the vineyard now is, they were sure it was 'the place'. Daughter Christy planted the classic three varieties of Chardonnay, Pinot Noir and Pinot Meunier in 2019 (they buy their Pinot Gris grapes in), with the sympathetic renovations of the Oast House and the conversion of an old barn into the tasting room, winery and distillery happening two years later.

A gorgeous mouse motif features on the labels of both the wines and spirits – the original, designed by Sir Basil Spence, who worked on Canterbury Cathedral, is on the Mousehall Oast House – along with a striking medieval hexafoil, a six-petal protective symbol or daisy wheel used to ward off witches and evil spirits, which was also found on the house.

Whilst the elegant yet juicy wines are made by her parents, the distillery is Christy's domain and the spirits are fantastic. Back in South Africa she used to manage a five-star safari lodge in the bush, where nightly G&T sundowners were par for the course and, seeing how popular gin was in England, started this side of the business. The spirits carry the name Mousehall whilst the wines are labelled Tidebrook, after a brook that runs through the property. A bountiful botanical garden provides for the spirits, there are hives – apparently English bees are much friendlier than South African ones! – for honey, and Dorper sheep trim the vineyard grass. I'd struggle to think of a nicer spot to spend an afternoon.

The Wines

Currently only still wines are made, though a sparkling rosé is on the lees, with more bubbles planned for the future.

MEDIEVAL MONK PINOT GRIS VINTAGE+
pear, honeysuckle, juicy — ££

SADDLE STONE CHARDONNAY VINTAGE+
elegant, citrus, spice — £££

SIX PETALS ROSÉ VINTAGE+
delicate, crunchy, cranberry — ££

THE TIPPING POINT PINOT NOIR VINTAGE+
sappy, fragrant, red berries — £££

The Spirits

Christy is also working on an apple brandy, a brandy, vermouth and absinthe and there is an elderflower apéritif too.

SUSSEX DRY GIN
vanilla, verbena, coriander, cardamom **££££**

CITRUS VODKA
tangerine, grapefruit, orange, lemon **££££**

BARREL-AGED GIN
hazelnut, toast, spice **£££**

Tours & tastings

Tours and tastings run throughout the year. There is a wine tour and tasting and a spirit one, or the two can be combined. Booking essential.

Eating

Local cheese, charcuterie and homemade biltong, with a pizza oven for private events.

Good to know

Stay at the six-person Oast House (with hot tub, honesty bar and pre-mixed negronis). Nearby vineyards include Wildwood, Birchden, Beacon Down, Oastbook, Mountfield, Hidden Spring and Balfour.

Oastbrook Vineyard

A quirky base for exploring the Rother Wine Triangle

Arguably best known for having a distinctive Hobbit House that guests can stay in, Nick Brewer and Brazilian wife America (she was born on 4 July) bought their traditional oast house and surrounding land – that used to be an old Guinness hop farm – with no intention of growing grapes whatsoever. But on moving in, America decided to grow some vines up the outside walls to remind her of her childhood home in Bahia, with a healthy crop soon following. Rather unexpectedly, this turned out to be the very start of their wine journey, as with some encouragement from local growers whose brains she'd been picking, she enrolled at Plumpton College.

Whilst there, she interrogated Oastbrook's *terroir* a bit more. It turned out that the south-facing site with clay, silt and sandstone soils was ideal for growing grapes; indeed, the heavier soils would add texture and weight to their still wines. They took the plunge and the first vines were planted in 2018.

Of the estate's sixty-five acres, eighteen are now under vine: Pinot Noir (777 clone), Pinot Meunier and Chardonnay (both Champagne and Burgundy clones), as well as Pinot Gris and Pinot Blanc (Alsatian clones). Initially the plan was to make sparkling wines, but they spotted a gap in the market for still and now make both, although the emphasis is on their easy-drinking whites. Their first vintage was in 2020.

America is clearly most at home in the vineyard and is passionate about biodiversity and sustainability, following organic principles as much as possible, encouraging natural wildflower growth and keeping bees. Nick, meanwhile, also went to Plumpton College and is now the winemaker, with everything being done on site by the two of them.

The Wines

Nick is in charge of the wines, with the majority being still.

SPARKLING ROSÉ VINTAGE
hawthorn, cranberry, redcurrant £££

PINOT BLANC VINTAGE+
pear, honeysuckle, melon ££

WHITE PINOT NOIR VINTAGE+
subtle, red apples, raspberry ££

Tours & tastings

Tours and tastings run all year round, predominantly at the weekends, with a Vineyard Tour & Tasting in the summer and a Winter Winery Tour & Tasting too. In the summer holidays Kids' Tours are run by their daughter, Gabby. The large tasting room is also open for informal tastings. Look out for their annual Brazilian-inspired summer party by the pool, Harvest Days and a *sabrage* event. Wine club.

Eating

Cheese and charcuterie boards are available.

Good to know

Stay at the Round Door Cottage (aka the Hobbit House) for a special experience. Also on site is Avalon Waterside Lodge, as well as luxury glamping, with a rustic wooden bar nearby, proper loos and a shower. There are also plenty of neighbouring wineries to visit, such as Mountfield Winery and Sedlescombe Organic.

Oxney Organic Estate

The artisan producer making single-estate wines

'Eco is everything,' explains Kristin Syltevik, the warm and wonderfully no-nonsense Norwegian proprietor, who along with her partner, Paul Dobson, are the owners of Oxney Organic near Rye. She is the living, breathing embodiment of her beliefs and lifestyle, and imbues the entire estate with a sense of *kos* (a bit like *hygge*), a Norwegian word that means contentment and enjoying simple, often outdoor activities.

Looking to start something new after a successful career in tech PR, Kristin toyed with the idea of growing herbs before landing on viticulture, starting the vineyard in 2012, assisted by viticultural expert Stephen Skelton MW. Although she was advised that growing grapes organically would result in yields too low to be commercial, she was determined to press ahead. Organic was a personal philosophy and if she couldn't grow the grapes organically, she wouldn't do it at all.

But through careful canopy management, being 'vigilant and super-detailed', as well as spraying herbal teas on the vines (such as chamomile and fennel), she produces healthy, ripe grapes from their thirty-five acres of Chardonnay, Pinot Noir, Pinot Meunier and Seyval Blanc, located in the High Weald Area of Outstanding Natural Beauty. Each grape variety is planted with different clones, which gives them a wide range of base wines to play with in the winery, and so everything is picked, pressed and kept separately to ensure that their wines are unique and interesting. With lots of exciting plans underway to enhance the guest experience at Oxney, there's never been a better time to visit this wonderful winery.

The Wines

The award-winning organic wines are made by Kristin and consultant Salvatore Leone. Unsurprisingly, her approach in the winery is sustainable and low intervention, using wild ferments with minimal fining, filtration and sulphur, as well as solar panels and wood chips.

OXNEY CLASSIC VINTAGE*
bready, toasty, nutty, lovely — £££

OXNEY ROSÉ NV
fresh, crunchy, raspberry, red apples — ££

OXNEY ROSÉ VINTAGE+
ballerina pink, strawberries, cherry blossom — ££

Tours & tastings
The focus is on small, intimate and personal tours, with tastings and wine flights running during the winter and tours and tastings on weekends in high season. Wine club.

Eating
Local cheeses, charcuterie, smoked fish and homemade pickles. No plastics; everything is reusable, with wicker baskets sourced from Somerset for vineyard picnics.

Good to know
Two vineyard-based shepherd's huts (the Hunt and the Dobson) are available to rent, as is the Vineyard House or, in nearby Stone-cum-Ebony, are the Oxney Barns, of which there are three. Tillingham (a biodynamic wine estate) is just over ten minutes away and Kristin runs the vineyard there too.

Rathfinny

The estate that pioneered Sussex PDO

Before the first vines had even been planted, a huge amount of hype had been whipped up surrounding this hugely ambitious project. Step forward Mark Driver, a former hedge-fund manager who, on deciding to leave the City at the relatively young age of forty-six was looking for another concern. Whilst helping his eldest daughter research university courses, he stumbled across Plumpton College (going on to sponsor the Rathfinny Research Winery there) and thought that wine and winemaking sounded fascinating, enrolling on the course. Inspired by the still quite fledgling industry, he and his wife Sarah decided to embark upon a fairly bold plan for a wine estate, and in 2010 they bought Rathfinny, so called because an Irish family called Finny had bought the farm in the 1800s, with 'rath' being the Celtic word for a homestead.

They chose the site because of the south-facing, silty clay loam soils over chalk, with the first fifty acres of vines being planted in 2012. Winds blow in from the sea – with views down to the coast you can see the Seven Sisters and Cuckmere Haven beach – and so a fairly extensive tree-planting project (to provide wind breaks, although even they needed protecting!) went hand in hand with planting the vines. A mix of Burgundian and Champagne clones of the classic three varieties went in: Chardonnay, Pinot Noir and Pinot Meunier with a sprinkling of Pinot Gris too. Of the 600-acre estate, 230 are now under vine, with the wines being Pinot Noir-dominant.

Situated as they are in the South Downs National Park, Rathfinny are part of the Countryside Stewardship scheme and so sustainability is a something of a given. Legumes (such as clover) are planted over 130 acres to help with nitrogen fixing and soil health and, rather wonderfully, they use falcons (peregrine and merlin) to scare

off the pigeons, crows and seagulls rather than plastic netting. The B Corp winery – awarded B Corporation Certification (by B Lab) when certain social and environmental standards are met – even has a beautiful roof meadow, home to visiting skylarks.

The Drivers knew that getting visitors on site was going to be an important part of their business. They wanted to share the excitement that world-class wines are being made in Sussex, pushing for the creation of the Sussex PDO, so that people would be able to walk into a bar in Hong Kong and ask for a glass of 'Sussex' rather than a glass of Champagne. Luckily, you don't have to go across the world to be able to do that but can sip on a glass of Sussex in situ instead.

The Wines

Still wines are branded Cradle Valley, with only the sparkling being Rathfinny.

CRADLE VALLEY PINOT GRIS VINTAGE+
juicy, pear, apricot, melon — £

CLASSIC CUVÉE VINTAGE
red apple, lemon meringue, almond — £££

ROSÉ VINTAGE
elegant, summer berries, cranberry, raspberry — ££££

BLANC DE NOIRS VINTAGE*
cherry blossom, mixed-berry pavlova — £££££

Tours & tastings

Cellar door open seven days a week, with complimentary drop-in tastings. Vineyard trail with map all year round. Tours and tastings run throughout the year; either a summer (more vineyard-focused) or winter one. Weddings, private and corporate events.

Eating

The Flint Barns dining room serves dinner, Sunday lunch and pop-up summer events. There are also collaborations with other restaurants and chefs. The Hut (their al fresco wine bar) is open from spring to early autumn, serving wines, snacks, light bites and hot drinks.

Good to know

Stay at one of the ten en-suite rooms at the Flint Barns B&B or the self-catering, dog-friendly Rathfinny Cottage. Bikes. Explore Wealden Wine Trail. About thirty minutes to Henners.

Ridgeview

One of the original English estates

Mike Roberts MBE will for ever be remembered as being one of the true founding fathers of the English wine industry. In the 1990s he bought some land with his wife, Chris, just outside Ditchling, with sweeping views across to the South Downs Ridge, naming the estate Ridgeview in honour of this distinctive vista. The first vines were planted in 1995 and to the classic three varieties: Chardonnay, Pinot Noir and Pinot Meunier on clay, clay loam and loam soils.

From the outset his intention was always to make traditional method sparkling wines when this was still very much in its infancy. Nyetimber may have started planting their vines in 1988, but their first wine – a Blanc de Blancs – wasn't released until 1996 (to great acclaim), the year after the Roberts's had started planting. Emulating the wines of Champagne at this time was still very much uncharted territory, but Mike was ambitious and determined, not just for his own winery but for the wider English industry. He played a huge role in raising its profile and was one of the first to sell his wine into the supermarkets, introducing them to a wider consumer base. He was awarded an MBE for his services to the English wine industry in 2011, a few years before he passed away in 2014 aged seventy-one.

Son Simon Roberts is the winemaker at Ridgeview and has been since 1998, and he explains that the house style is one that is intended to evoke the English countryside, with flavours of green apple, hedgerow and blossom. The wines are appealing and fresh, and go hand in hand with Ridgeview's philosophy that 'life is for celebrating'. Until recently, Simon's sister Tamara was CEO for over twenty years, spearheading an enormous period of growth and understanding the importance of tourism, opening the winery to visitors and setting up their excellent restaurant. She very much took over where Mike left off and continued to build it into one of the most recognisable and loved English brands in the market.

The Wines

Wines are mainly sparkling (there is a still rosé and Chardonnay), with the sparkling pinks being amongst my all-time favourites.

BLOOMSBURY NV
green apple, lemon sherbet, honeysuckle, nuts £££

FITZROVIA ROSÉ NV*
zippy, redcurrant, raspberry, Eton Mess £££

ROSÉ DE NOIRS VINTAGE*
cherry bakewell, raspberry, strawberry £££££

Tours & tastings

Guided wine tastings, Classic Tour & Wine Tasting, Winter Cellar Tour, self-guided audio tour (outside, free). Private and corporate tours, tastings and events. Wine club.

Eating

The Ridgeview Wine Bar and Shop offers light bites and boards, whilst the contemporary The Rows & Vine restaurant, which overlooks the Chardonnay vines, is a stunning seasonal (spring to early autumn) offering with three 'pods'. Family-friendly.

Good to know

Lots of other wineries to explore locally, with these all being reachable in under ten minutes: Artelium, Court Garden, Everflyht and Sugrue South Downs.

Sugrue South Downs

Cult wines from winemaking legend Dermot Sugrue

For those in the wine trade, Dermot needs little in the way of introduction, as his name is inexorably tied to some of the most historic and awarded English wineries – including, now, his own – but for those who haven't heard of him, let me introduce you to this talented, likeable Irishman.

Whilst studying at Plumpton College, Dermot worked at Nyetimber as their assistant winemaker, quickly advancing to the position of winemaker before meeting Pip and Harry Goring in 2005. They were thinking of planting vines and building a winery at what was to become Wiston Estate, on a swathe of South Downs chalk. This piqued Dermot's imagination to such an extent that he ultimately jumped ship, joining Pip and Harry in their new venture the following year. He also planted his own small vineyard at Storrington Priory, from which he was to make his inaugural wine, 'The Trouble With Dreams', made at Wiston from 2009 vintage fruit, released in 2013.

The intriguing name of his first fizz revolves rather wonderfully around the story of a monastic order of Catholic priests who wondered whether their land might be suitable for vines. As a consequence, Father Paul McMahon got in touch, and it was agreed that Dermot would make wine for them, but that he could keep some of the crop with which to make his own wine. But the grapes were so ripe that the whole harvest was eaten by birds, ruining any hope of a 2008 vintage. To which the Father murmured 'That's the trouble with dreams' – thus naming Dermot's wine before it was even made.

The lure to devote himself to making his own wines full-time proved to be irresistible, and with his wife Ana's encouragement (an extremely experienced and accomplished winemaker in her own right) and some high-profile investment from the likes of Robin Hutson OBE (who set up The Pig hotels), actor Huge Bonneville and chef Angela Hartnett, he left Wiston to set up Sugrue. The Bee Tree vineyard was planted in May 2023 and the tractor barn next to it was converted into a new winery, filled with second-hand equipment including barrels (nicknamed the 'ladies' by Dermot) which were shipped over from France, and a disco ball.

The Wines

Dermot and Ana's wines sell out fast with a richly deserved reputation for both quality and sheer drinkability. A pioneer of using oak on sparkling base blends as well as crafting quirky whites and opulent reds, these are wines not to be missed.

THE TROUBLE WITH DREAMS MV*
rich, savoury, nuts, tarte tatin — ££££

SPARKLING ROSÉ EX MACHINA VINTAGE*
pomegranate, raspberry, cranberry — £££££

BONKERS V2 CHARDONNAY+*
varnish, spice, citrus, lovely — ££

Tours & tastings
A monthly Winemaker Masterclass and a limited number of guided tours and tastings.

Eating
Sugrue Sundays – a series of al fresco pop-up lunches – run over the summer.

Good to know
This is a very rural winery, so follow the bumpy track past slightly dilapidated farm buildings and keep on going until you reach it.

Tillingham

Enjoy natural wines at this fabulous countryside retreat near Rye

For many years Ben Walgate was the poster boy for English natural wines, having stepped down from his role as CEO at Gusbourne in 2016 to pursue a long-held dream of starting something more eclectic of his own. This was made possible when Lord and Lady Devonport – who shared his interests in the environment and sustainability – leased him an old, derelict farm on their Peasmarsh Place Estate.

Set amongst seventy acres, the first vines were planted in 2018, with more going in the following year, and now over twenty different grape varieties are grown on twenty acres. These include Chardonnay, Pinot Noir, Pinot Meunier and Pinot Noir Précoce, but also Bacchus, Ortega, Siegerrebe, Dornfelder, Regent and Manzoni Bianco: a mix of classic varieties, PIWIs and experimental varieties for England, such as Gamay. The remaining land is left fallow.

After about five years, Ben left to concentrate on his own wine label, Walgate & Co., based in Rye, and with his departure a new consultant winemaker started, Salvatore Leone, who, alongside amiable head of wine Tierney Beames has ushered in a subtle new style. The range has been streamlined, with predominantly still wines being made, and the goal is simply to make 'stable, consistent and delicious' wines, by following a slightly more pragmatic approach. Nevertheless, Tierney assures me that 'experimentation is here to stay' with an impressive range of winemaking vessels – qvevri, clay and concrete – on display but that Tillingham's principles have to go hand in hand with being practical. The winery is also in conversion so that it can be certified biodynamic – the vineyards already are.

Arguably, the jewel in the crown at Tillingham is not just its wines but its on-site offering, which is absurdly gorgeous and aesthetically pleasing, encouraging guests to stay for that bit longer. A whole weekend can easily be whiled away here, imbibing the wines, eating at the restaurant, enjoying the viewing deck or the walled garden before staying overnight in a stylish bell tent or en-suite room. A very special place indeed.

The Wines

A reset in 2023 means that slightly more commercial wines are being made, which are still low intervention.

COL VINTAGE
clementine, baked apple, citrus, stone fruit **££**

QVEVRI ORTEGA VINTAGE+*
juicy, herbal, quince **£££**

R STILL RED NV+
rosehip, pepper, balsamic strawberries **££**

Tours & tastings

Run throughout the year, with more at the weekends and in the summer. Larger groups require a private tour, by arrangement. Pop-up creative events such as screen printing, ceramics, floristry and ice baths. Harvest festival. Wedding receptions. Shop. Corporate events. A little storage room offers a flexible space for small tastings.

Eating

A Michelin Green Star restaurant sources food from the farm and their own walled garden. Private dining room.

No children under twelve at dinner but very welcome in the Pizza Barn (a converted Dutch barn), the bar - which offers smaller sharing plates - and for Sunday lunch. Child-friendly events are also run. No dogs in the restaurant or bar. Book a Gourmet Getaway: room, dinner and breakfast.

Good to know

There are eleven hotel rooms (four are dog-friendly) and two bell tents (with vineyard view and log burners, available in the spring and summer). Oxney Organic is just over ten minutes away and Chapel Down in Kent under twenty.

West Sussex

Albourne Estate

Tasty wines and spectacular South Downs views

After having her second child, Alison Nightingale left her old corporate life behind and enrolled at Plumpton College part time to 'find out more about wine and winemaking', and discovered that she loved it. Four years later, with a degree under her belt and a marked interest in the wider growth of the industry, and in particular what Eric Heerema was doing at Nyetimber, she decided to look for a site.

Frustratingly, this proved trickier than expected, as there were a number of boxes that needed to be ticked, most importantly wanting to live on site, which meant it had to be child-friendly. But after three years, despite having looked in both Devon and Cornwall, Albourne Farm came on to the market whilst the family was living in nearby Hurstpierpoint. The sale was completed in 2009, with the first vines being planted the following year – Chardonnay, Pinot Noir, Pinot Meunier, Bacchus, Pinot Gris, Ortega, Dornfelder and Pinot Blanc on sandy loam soils.

Wines are made on site using only estate-grown fruit and Alison is markedly passionate about sustainability: the winery is solely powered by renewable energy (largely made possible by their solar panels), they embrace regenerative viticulture, and have employed an ambitious tree-planting scheme which has seen many thousands of trees go into the ground. Their goal is to become a carbon-neutral producer.

Since Covid, their hospitality offering has increased enormously, with many visitors coming from across the country to enjoy a relaxed cellar-door experience, with breathtaking views over the vines from their expansive balcony.

The Wines

Alison makes her excellent, great-value wines with consultant Salvatore Leone. Production is roughly 50:50 still to sparkling.

BLANC DE BLANCS VINTAGE* elegant, grilled nuts, marzipan, croissant	£££
BACCHUS VINTAGE+* grapefruit, lime, zingy, lemons	£
SUSSEX ROSÉ MV+* pale, dry, delicate, crunchy, redcurrant	£

Tours & tastings

Plenty of options during the spring and summer, including a Wine Tasting Experience, self-guided wine flight or walking trail (complete with booklet and posts around the vineyard) or the full vineyard tour with wine and cheese. Alternatively, just drop in for a glass of wine after a dog walk. Birthday parties and hen groups welcome, as are tour groups courtesy of Great British Wine Tours and Shuttle & Vine.

Eating

Simple food platters and a weekly supper club in the summer, with a rotating offering of pop-up food vendors.

Good to know

There is a raft of other local wineries to visit, including Bolney, Court Garden, Everflyht, Artelium and Ridgeview.

Ambriel Sparkling

Elegant, 'unapologetically English' sparklers

After being burgled at their London home, barrister Wendy Outhwaite KC and her husband Charles popped the cork on a 'restorative' bottle of bubbles – which turned out to be Nyetimber – and were amazed. Already passionate about wine and having studied to the Wine & Spirit Education Trust (WSET) Level 3, they found themselves, admittedly a bit 'starry-eyed', thinking that this was something they could do themselves, and so the search for a site started in earnest.

After hiring lots of different consultants, who all disagreed with each other, they initially concentrated on Cornwall and Kent, but five years later they saw the ideal house with land and a derelict barn advertised in the *Chichester Observer*. In 2008, on completion, they planted about twenty-three acres with Burgundian clones of Chardonnay, Pinot Noir and Pinot Meunier on greensand rock soils, even finding ancient coins from 64 BCE on the property: there used to be a river there and when it started to run dry, coins were thrown in and wishes made to try and keep it flowing. Fossils were also discovered, suggesting that the land was historically a Neanderthal hunting site.

Keen supporters of sustainability, Wendy and Charles have solar panels, farm regeneratively, eschew chemicals whenever possible and have a flock of Ouessant sheep to control grass growth between rows; being the smallest sheep in the world, they are very light and don't damage the vines. The climate at Pulborough is a 'goldilocks' one, not too hot and not too cold, and the site benefits from no frost and a long growing season, which helps to build phenolic (colour, flavour and tannin) ripeness. Wines are made from estate fruit only and they have always been made on site. Ambriel initially employed two winemakers, but after attending Plumpton College, Charles is in charge of the primary ferment, vinifying – winemaking – by clone to keep them separate, and Wendy the blending, which is always done blind; not knowing which component is which. They tend not to put their wines through MLF – they feel you lose more than you gain – but love long lees ageing, as it helps temper acidity whilst retaining freshness.

The Ambriel name itself is an amalgamation of two angels, Ambrosia and Gabriel, with the angel symbol referring to the wines being 'unapologetically English' – in many languages the words for 'English' and 'angel' are very similar, and there is also a British flag on the foil. The colourway of dark green, silver and purple is a nod both to the suffragettes and Wendy's background in human-rights law. As with everything here, the branding has been done with intelligence coupled with a keen sense of humour – on the approach to the winery there is a road sign that reads 'Ambriel Close', a little joke that you will shortly be arriving at this rather delicious destination.

The Wines

Elegant sparkling wines made by Wendy and Charles.

CLASSIC MV
apples, pecans, bakery notes **££**

WENDLING BLANC DE BLANCS VINTAGE
green apples, apple Danish, lemon sherbet **£££**

HUZZAH ROSÉ MV*
lovely colour, petals, raspberry, berries **£££**

ENGLISH RESERVE DEMI-SEC MV

floral, lemon, quince **£££**

Tours & tastings

Run all year round: choose between a tasting or a tour and tasting, most of which are hosted by Wendy. Private tours available. Select pop-up and musical events too. Also a wine club: the Fizzicist (by the case) or Sipsters (bottle).

Eating

A chef can be hired for private events, with a dining table in the tasting barn.

Good to know

Lots of other local wineries around Pulborough to visit, including Nyetimber, Nutbourne, Stopham, Kinsbrook and Wiston. Children and dogs welcome.

Ashling Park Estate

A first-class, multifaceted experience

The approach to Ashling Park Estate is so grand, with its ornate gates and sweeping drive, that owner Gail Gardner was worried that it was intimidating potential customers, so she popped a café sign next to those gilded gates to reassure guests that it is open for all – which it very much is. The estate itself dates back to 1822 and was gifted by the nation to Lord Portal, who was Chief of the Air Staff and a key adviser to Winston Churchill, after his crucial role in helping to win World War II, before being bought by Gail's parents, Barrie and Janet Christie. She then persuaded her parents to let her plant vines in the hay meadow, or, as she says, 'what was essentially their front garden' after spending time in the Valais region of Switzerland and falling in love with vineyards and wine.

Viticulture specialists VineWorks advised on what should go where, with planting starting in May 2017, with Chardonnay, Pinot Noir and Pinot Meunier going in alongside Bacchus and Pinot Noir Précoce, covering ten acres of loam over chalk soils. Alongside the vines are some 200-year-old oak trees, and a beautiful lake is in the grounds too, which helps moderate temperature.

From the outset, Gail knew that she needed a route to market and wanted to offer experiences such as tours, tastings, a restaurant and corporate offerings; with Goodwood nearby they aren't short of smart car-enthusiast clients. Add in luxury lodges and a gin school, and you have everything on hand that you could possibly need for an unforgettable weekend away at this superior Sussex staycation.

The Wines

Wines aren't made on site but favour long lees ageing.

CUVÉE NV
apple crumble, nuts, muffin — **£££**

BLANC DE BLANCS VINTAGE
almond croissant, citrus, apple blossom — **£££**

ESTATE SELECTION PINOT NOIR VINTAGE+*
spicy, mocha, chocolate, cherries — **££**

Tours & tastings

Available all year round, with the tastings taking place in the Experience Room. There is also a fabulous Gin School with its own dedicated space. A calendar of events runs throughout the year such as Paint & Sip and a Harvest Experience. Cocktail-making classes.

Eating

The airy Vineyard Restaurant opened in 2021, with vine views from the balcony. The Portal Room offers private dining. Also a café, shop and cellar door and in the summer there is a silver Airstream bus bar outside.

Good to know

Five lodges, with one being fully wheelchair accessible, are named after the stages of the vine cycle (such as Budburst), with log burners and sunset views. Along with the main building, they were designed by Will Hardie of Channel 4's *Amazing Spaces*, with both the accommodation and restaurant being dog-friendly. Tinwood is fifteen minutes away.

Bolney Wine Estate

The heritage estate with an impressive hospitality focus

Originally named Bookers Vineyard, Bolney Wine Estate is steeped in English wine history, being the sixth-oldest commercial vineyard in the country. Rodney and Janet Pratt bought the land – an old smallholding and chicken farm – in 1972, planting vines the following year and putting in three acres of Germanic grape variety Müller-Thurgau. More vines went in over the years – they were one of the first to 'trial' Chardonnay and Pinot Noir, which were fairly revolutionary then – with their Plumpton College-educated daughter Sam Linter coming on board in 1995. Under her direction, the winery saw a significant period of expansion and quality improvements, including changing the name and pioneering the production of English red wine.

Never ones to rest on their laurels, changes continued to be made with further plantings, including the Eighteen Acre Vineyard, a new winery (later expanded and opened by Queen Camilla), and a small visitor centre. In January 2022 Bolney was bought by the world's largest sparkling-wine group Henkell Freixenet, who were keen to get a foothold in England's exciting industry. Perhaps not surprisingly, whilst production used to favour still wines over sparkling (around 60:40), the focus is slowly moving more towards sparkling wines.

Previously there was a fairly limited offering in terms of the visitor experience, but the new owners saw the opportunity in wine tourism, and developed the site, making it relaxed, inviting and inclusive, with a light, bright and airy restaurant with lots of windows, a café and wine bar, shop and state-of-the-art tasting rooms.

The Wines

Miguel Symington has taken over the winemaking, having recently moved from Rathfinny, with the sparkling wines singing.

BOLNEY BUBBLY NV
rhubarb, custard, pineapple, tasty — ££

CLASSIC CUVÉE NV
golden apples, lemon sherbet, nuts — £££

BLANC DE BLANCS VINTAGE
elegant, citrus, frangipane, apples — ££££

Tours & tastings

Rolling hospitality with 'friendly and accessible' events. Drop in cellar-door tastings (throughout the week at the welcome desk), a Pairing Tour & Tasting and the Bolney Experience Tour & Tasting. Tasting in the Vines (summer only). Seasonal events such as Mother's Day bottle painting, Harvest Experience, Festive Fridays and Twilight Tours. Wonderful wedding reception location. Wine club.

Eating

Upstairs is the Eighteen Acre restaurant, with vine views from the balcony. Chef's experiences, afternoon teas and Sunday roasts. Private dining space. Wine flights at the downstairs café and wine bar, which is dog-friendly.

Good to know

Highweald Wine Estate is under ten minutes away, Albourne is close by, too, as are Leonardslee and Ridgeview. Brighton is half an hour away.

Digby Fine English

I first came across these wines when at a local 'Bubbles and Botanicals' fair in Sussex and was blown away by the whole range. There are five fizzes, two non-vintage (the Brut NV was the first English fizz to be served on British Airways business class) and three vintage offerings. Named by husbands and co-owners American Trevor Clough and Jason Humphries after seventeenth-century scientist Sir Kenelm Digby, who is credited with inventing the modern wine bottle, Digby offers guided tastings of their fabulous wines in their Arundel tasting room. This quaint castle town is also very close to Wiston, ensuring a delightful day out.

Highweald Wine Estate

When my lovely neighbours got married a couple of years ago, they served Highweald Brut Reserve NV at the reception and I thought it was really rather good – and good value too. They also make a sparkling rosé NV and a Blanc de Noirs Vintage and also a few still wines: a white blend, a couple of Chardonnays (including a wild ferment) and a still rosé. Grapes are grown on chalky soils across three sites – Highweald, Lake Street and Alder Ridge. Ten minutes from Haywards Heath train station in the pretty village of Ansty, this is a seriously stunning spot. The grounds and gardens have been designed by Andy Sturgeon, who has won many awards at the RHS Chelsea Flower Show, and the wooden decking outside the garden bar offers expansive views over the vines. 'Unpretentious' tours and tastings run at weekends.

Kinsbrook

The funky, family-friendly producer

The idea of planting a vineyard on the family farm was one that had been percolating since 2006, but it wasn't until Joe Beckett, at the time a semi-professional rugby player, returned from New Zealand at the age of twenty-one that it started to come to fruition. After experiencing the wine industry over there, and in particular the tourism side, he was inspired not just to plant a vineyard and make wines, but also to include a hospitality offering.

Soils were heavy, with clay underneath, and needed draining, with the land drains feeding the brook at the bottom of the vineyard, inspiring the name Kinsbrook – kin (family) and the brook. Planting started in 2017 and some 44,500 vines are now planted over three sites in West Chiltington, including the Picketty site, where the winery and farmhouse are found. Varieties include Chardonnay, Pinot Noir, Pinot Meunier, Pinot Blanc, Bacchus and Ortega.

The first wines were released in 2020, during the pandemic, with the bird logo on the bottles being a red-billed chough, a crow-like bird with a red beak and feet, which has the nickname Becket (the same as their surname, minus a letter 't') due to it being used on the coat of arms of Thomas Becket. Wines are fresh and playful: approachable, easy-drinking and enjoyable, with Joe encapsulating the 'new-wave winemaker' who wants to experiment. He explains that he has full licence to do so, which helps him to 'get the very best out of each parcel' of fruit and allows him to play around with different styles, such as the 'Chough au vin', a Beaujolais-esque red. Tasting out of tank in his brand-new winery, he was buzzing with ideas for new wines and different blending opportunities so that he can 'get the best complexity and depth from each wine'.

The Wines

Historically, wines were made off site (fizz by Dermot Sugrue and stills at Stopham), but with the new winery ready in 2025, the broad range of wines are now made by Joe.

NAUGHT ZERO DOSAGE VINTAGE
fresh, savoury, buttered toast, citrus — £££

ABC OAKED CHARDONNAY VINTAGE+
popcorn, spice, pear, apricot — £££

NIMBY PINOT NOIR RONDO MV+
dark, red cherries, boysenberry, soft — ££

Tours & tastings

The vibe here is relaxed, rustic and welcoming, with Joe's wife Rebecca Dancer running this must-visit estate with him. Public and private tours: private available at a time to suit, minimum two people. Public tours run at weekends, with a three-wine tasting. Wine Chatter wine club. Seasonal events, including summer and harvest festivals.

Eating

The restaurant is open seven days a week, operating as a café early in the week and a restaurant at other times, offering seasonal small plates, steaks and roasts. Dog-friendly. Downstairs is a deli café (serving wine flights), cellar door and gift shop. Outdoor seating. In the summer there is a sourdough pizza shed and the Pink Bar. Supper clubs.

Good to know

Family-friendly with a small playground.

Leonardslee Family Vineyards

Fine sparkling wines, Michelin dining, sculpture and golf

The story of Penny Streeter OBE is an almost impossibly impressive one: a journey that takes her from being homeless and living in a shelter with three young children, following the collapse of both her marriage and business, to a multimillionaire. Despite the failure of her first business, she launched a second one – a nursing-staff agency – with her mother Marion, moving the back-end part of the business to South Africa, where she fell in love not just with wine but with wine hospitality, buying Benguela Cove Lagoon Wine Estate in the Western Cape in 2013. Shortly afterwards she purchased Mannings Heath Golf Club and the beautiful 240-acre Leonardslee Lakes & Gardens, both in West Sussex.

The two properties are a short drive away from each other and offer different guest experiences. The vast majority of the vineyard acreage – thirty-seven acres on clay soils – were planted at Mannings Heath, also known as Leonardslee Wine Estate, in 2017, predominantly with Chardonnay, along with Pinot Noir and Pinot Meunier. There are just four acres of vines at the gardens, but these include ten rows of Pinotage – the only ones in England – grown for colour for the rosé and a nod to their ongoing and close relationship with South Africa.

At the moment, three terrific vintage sparkling wines are made (the Blanc de Blancs is my favourite), with the barn swallow emblem being chosen to grace all of the bottles because it is a bird that migrates annually from Sussex to Africa. Inspired by the wine tourism there, Penny's ultimate aim is to turn Leonardslee into 'a world-class wine destination'. Given that Leonardslee Family Vineyards was ranked fifty-sixth in the 2025 World's Best Vineyards competition, they are well on their way.

The Wines

South African winemaker Johann Fourie makes the wines in both hemispheres, with the English fizz currently being made at Wiston.

BRUT RESERVE VINTAGE
apple strudel, nutmeg, blossom, citrus **£££**

BLANC DE BLANCS VINTAGE*
spice, hazelnut, apple, bread **£££££**

BRUT ROSÉ VINTAGE
cherry clafoutis, raspberry, strawberry **£££**

Tours & tastings

Wine experiences are offered at both sites, with most being at Mannings Heath. Tutored Tastings, a Vineyard Tour & Tutored Tasting (includes hopping on a golf buggy and sometimes *sabrage*) or a self-guided wine flight in the tasting room. Harvest days and seasonal events. Function room for weddings, private or corporate events. Golf course. Sparkling wine masterclass at the gardens.

Eating

The Vineyard Kitchen is at Mannings Heath, as is the Spike Bar. Summer BBQs on the terrace. Try the top-notch tasting menu at the Michelin-starred Interlude restaurant at the gardens. Vineyard Picnic. The Clocktower Café.

Good to know

The nine-bedroom, dog-friendly Vineyard Hotel is based at the (very pink!) Mannings Heath Golf Club, whereas the Grade II listed Leonardslee House is at the exceptional gardens and has ten luxurious rooms.

Nutbourne Vineyards

A charming, authentic, single-estate vineyard

In all honesty, Nutbourne wasn't really on my radar, but given that they are located in the 'vineyard mecca' of Pulborough, I thought I'd pop in whilst in the environs, and I'm so glad that I did, as the wines are excellent! Owners Peter and Bridget Gladwin have been at Nutbourne for over thirty-five years, bringing their family here in 1991. At the time, Peter worked in hospitality and had two restaurants (since sold) but is now chairman of the Gladwin Restaurant Group. His artist wife Bridget, meanwhile – whose striking, colourful works adorn both the wine labels and walls here – looks after the viticulture side of things. They have three sons, Gregory, Oliver and Richard, and all are involved in the business. Gregory is based at Nutbourne and is the winemaker and a farmer, helping to grow the food in the polytunnel that supplies the picnics and platters. Richard and Oliver run the Local & Wild restaurants, with Oliver being a trained chef and, it appears, something of an artist too – his oyster label is found on their still blush wine.

The vineyard had historically been planted to Germanic varieties as early as 1979, but over the years French ones were also added to the mix, with a selection of different clones of Chardonnay, Pinot Noir and Pinot Meunier going in – on greensand over sandstone soils – as well as Pinot Blanc and Pinot Gris. There are now twenty-four acres under vine, with some Bacchus, Huxelrebe and Reichensteiner remaining.

Over time a winery was built, and the listed derelict windmill (built in 1854) was also restored, and for a time became the cellar-door shop. However, it transpired that the walls were too thick for payment transactions, so that didn't work! It does, however, offer fabulous views across the vines to the South Downs and can be used as a private event space. There are over ten wines in the range and they are delicious, distinctive and affordable – I think you'd be hard pressed to find a better quality-to-cost ratio. Still wines are a fun balance of Germanic-based blends (such as the Sussex Reserve), an excellent Bacchus, blush and Pinot Noir. Sparkling wines are incredible value, especially the two Nutty wines. A great discovery.

The Wines

Gregory Gladwin makes the wines with consultant Emma Rice.

NUTTY WILD NV*
raspberry, cherry blossom, rhubarb ££

NUTTY BRUT VINTAGE*
rich, complex, apple crumble, toasted nuts ££

SUSSEX RESERVE VINTAGE+
citrus, honeysuckle, elderflower £

BLUSH VINTAGE+
pale, delicate, strawberry, rosehip £

PINOT NOIR VINTAGE+*
spice, oak, mocha, red plums, chocolate ££

Tours & tastings
The cellar door is open throughout the week. Vineyard trail (with map, don't miss the alpacas), and in summer there are wine flights (three wines) with tasting notes. Tours run at the weekend throughout spring and summer. Can add

on a platter or picnic. Wine Lodge to sit by the vines. Windmill views. Wooden viewing deck. Private tours available. Weddings.

Eating

Picnics and platters, Burgers & Bubbly at the Wine Lodge (select days in summer). Pop-up Farm Feasts in the vines. Private dining. Harvest specials. Off-site there is their Local & Wild restaurant chain, with five London outlets and their first in Sussex, the Black Horse in Amberley (with rooms).

Good to know

Lots of local wineries: Nyetimber, Stopham, Kinsbrook, Smock Alley (a co-operative, community vineyard) and Ambriel Sparkling.

Nyetimber

A luxury experience at an iconic winery

Nyetimber is the winery that put England on the world wine stage and, as such, it enjoys something of a fabled reputation. Stuart and Sandy Moss, two ambitious Americans from Chicago, bought the medieval estate in 1986 and even though they were advised, by the British Ministry of Agriculture no less, to plant apples as opposed to grapes, they went ahead and did it anyway. Flying in the face of conventional wisdom, they shunned the Germanic varieties typically grown at the time and planted the three French grapes best suited to making outstanding sparklers, something never done before, but they were confident that world-class sparkling wine could be made on these cool shores. Luckily, they proved all the naysayers wrong and their first vintage (1992) won a Gold medal at the IWSC, swiftly followed by their 1993 Classic Cuvée winning Best Sparkling Wine in the World, again at the IWSC. English sparkling wine had arrived!

The desire to return home, however, proved to be irresistible and so the Mosses sold up to Andy Hill (of 1980s band Bucks Fizz) and his wife, who sold it on again in 2006 to the current owner – Dutchman Eric Heerema. Eric promptly hired Canadian winemaker Cherie Spriggs and her husband, Brad Greatrix, who are still in charge of the wines today, with Cherie making headlines in 2025 when she won the IWC Sparkling Winemaker of the Year for a second time. That same year Nyetimber also took home the IWC Champion Sparkling Wine Trophy for their Blanc de Blancs 2016 (in magnum); the first time a producer from outside Champagne had ever won the award, with lots of column inches following such a remarkable achievement.

And Nyetimber's aim remains unchanged: to make the best English sparkling wine possible from their own fruit. Their vineyards cover over 1,050 acres, not just in Sussex but also Kent and Hampshire, with south-facing slopes sheltered by the Downs, on chalk or sandy soils. Overall, there are some 150 different parcels of land using different clones – both Champagne and Burgundy – and rootstocks, along with different vine ages (the 1988 Chardonnay plantings are some of the oldest in the country). This allows for an impressive 'artist's palette' of base wines from which to blend, ensuring complexity and layers of interest in the wines.

The estate's open days are still relatively nascent in terms of how long they have been running for, with them only taking place over a handful of weekends a year because this is actually Eric's family home. A highly polished yet accessible experience led by one of their brand ambassadors, this is a really special few hours in an exquisite setting that rather took me by surprise; an unparalleled chance to explore English winemaking history at an historic estate dating back to the Domesday Book. The experience would make an excellent gift.

The Wines

Nyetimber love long lees ageing for complexity, as well as using tiny amounts of oak, and they remain pioneers to this day; the first to market with both a demi-sec (Cuveé Chérie) and their premium 1086 wines – the first English fizz to retail at over £100 and, in fact, closer to £200 – but the focus on the open days is understandably their popular core range.

CLASSIC CUVÉE MV*
peanut brittle, apples, pastry, crème brûlée £££££

ROSE MV
rose-petal pink, raspberry, cherry, almond £££££

TILLINGTON SINGLE VINEYARD VINTAGE*
tarte tatin, nuts, shortbread £££££

Tours & tastings

Open days take place over select weekends in the summer, with multiple tours a day, typically. The ticket price (happily) is redeemable against a case of wine purchased on the day, at cellar-door prices. No dogs or children.

Eating

An exclusive 1086 'paired dining experience' is hosted at the estate over three weekends: in the spring, summer and autumn.

Good to know

Thomas Cromwell once lived at Nyetimber but it was given to Anne of Cleves following the annulment of her marriage to Henry VIII. Nutbourne Vineyards is on the very same lane and there are other wineries to explore locally too, from Wiston to Kinsbrook and Ambriel Sparkling.

Roebuck Estates

Come for the wines, stay for the view

Roebuck Estates might not be as well recognised as some of the larger players on the English sparkling scene but are fast gaining a reputation for excellence. Established when two friends purchased their first parcel of land in West Sussex in 2013, this has grown over time to include five other plots: three in Sussex, and two in Kent, all on well-drained greensand soils. Plantings were to the classic three Champagne varieties – Chardonnay, Pinot Noir and Pinot Meunier – with some Pinot Noir Précoce for the rosé.

Only vintage sparkling wines are produced, and the estates' emphasis has always been on quality whilst respecting sustainability, with a full-time ecologist on hand to advise on biodiversity. A pond is being put in at one of their vineyards, foils are plant-based, and the labels are water-based, so the entire bottle is recyclable. The wild roe deer that are seen in the vineyards, and after which the wines are named, are known for treading lightly on the land and Roebuck's goal is to do just that too.

The wines are united stylistically by extended lees ageing and bottle ageing, which helps make them attractive on release, as it helps soften acidity and keeps dosage low. The base blends are all partially fermented (30–40 per cent) in Burgundian oak, which adds layers of spice and complexity; it also helps temper acidity. The core range consists of a Classic Cuvée, a Rosé Reserve, a Rosé de Noirs and a Blanc de Noirs with the Rare Expressions range sitting above these.

This range showcases exceptional wines, largely displaying even longer lees ageing. They capture a moment, a variety or a place in time. Rare Expressions No. 19, for example, comes from block 19 in the Roman Villa vineyard, is from the 2015 vintage, uses the 667 clone of Pinot Noir and has eighty-four months lees ageing. Rare Expressions No. 96 is from the 2014 vintage and has ninety-six months of lees ageing. These wines are first class.

The Wines

There is no winery here, but the wines are expertly made off-site.

CLASSIC CUVÉE VINTAGE
elegant, apple turnover, nuts, citrus **£££**

ROSÉ DE NOIRS VINTAGE
pale colour, redcurrant, raspberry pip **££££**

BLANC DE NOIRS VINTAGE
grilled nuts, apples, cherry pastry **££££**

RARE EXPRESSIONS NO. 96*
poised, pecan pie, complex, impressive **£££££**

Tours & tastings

The tipi – known as the View – and bar were set up in 2024 so that tours and tastings could be offered in the spring and summer months, from April until harvest.

Eating

Nibbles and snacks from the tipi. In the summer, the Land Over, a pizza truck, can be found on site.

Good to know

A tasting room is being built for a year-round visitor experience. Dogs welcome – on leads – as are children (no leads required).

Stopham Estate

The rustic estate making delicious, drinkable whites

Winemaker and brand owner Simon Woodhead – who used to design automotive sensors for McLaren Formula 1 – had left engineering, moved to Madrid for three years and caught the 'wine bug'. On his return to England in 2004 he was determined to follow his dream of planting his own vineyard, so raised some capital, enrolled at Plumpton College and then – no mean feat – needed to find the right site.

As luck would have it, on his way to his friend Sarah's party in the village of Stopham, he drove past an empty (aside from a few rabbits), barren field that he thought looked ideal for vines. With Sarah's help he approached owner Sir Brian Barttelot – something of a wine lover himself – who agreed to lease him the land, along with an old barn that he could convert into a winery.

And so Stopham Estate vineyard was born: a fifteen-acre vineyard that is part of the wider 1,200-acre Stopham Estate, which has been in the same family – the Barttelots – since the fourteenth century. On a greensand ridge, it has poor, sandy soils – great for amplifying the aromatics of white grapes – and is south-facing with a low altitude. In 2007 Simon planted Pinot Gris (about 40 per cent of the vines), Pinot Blanc and Bacchus, with some Pinot Noir and Chardonnay for sparkling wines, favouring a sustainable approach. Unusually, about 85 per cent of his production is still white wines and that was always his passion and what he wanted to focus on: accessible, cool-fermented, aromatic whites, despite the sceptics. It's much harder to hide behind a bad vintage with still wines. Stopham has a small team, and Simon works with assistant winemaker and vineyard manager Adderley Pelly to create these extremely drinkable styles, made with 'precision and passion'.

The Wines

White wine specialists producing juicy, fruit-forward, hugely enjoyable wines.

BRUT VINTAGE
savoury, baked apples, nuts, citrus **£££**

PINOT GRIS VINTAGE+*
tropical, nectarine, quince, pear, mango **££**

BACCHUS VINTAGE+
lemon thyme, herbs, tomato leaf **££**

BARREL FERMENTED CHARDONNAY VINTAGE+
spiced apple, lemon peel, apricot **££**

Tours & tastings

High season (mid-spring to harvest), Saturdays only, taking in the vineyard, winery (a converted Grade II listed Victorian barn) and a tasting. Basic cellar door.

Eating

Nothing on site but can add on lunch at the White Hart pub, next to the River Arun and Stopham Bridge, or bring a picnic.

Good to know

Dogs and children welcome. Part of the emerging Arun and Adur wine cluster that includes wineries such as Ambriel Sparkling, Nutbourne, Kinsbrook, Smock Alley and Wiston.

Tinwood Estate

Sparkling wines with sunset views from romantic lodges

At the age of twenty-one, Art Tukker was given his family farm, where he was born, on the sole proviso that he could do anything with it – apart from continue to grow the iceberg lettuce that his family had been selling to the supermarkets since his Dutch dad bought the land in 1985. On taking it over in 2006, he decided to make the move from salad to vines, having written his final university dissertation, whilst studying agriculture, on 'The Future of English Wine' and appreciating that the West Sussex site near Chichester was sunny with well-drained flinty, chalk soils.

The initial twenty-eight acres of vines – Chardonnay, Pinot Noir, and Pinot Meunier – were planted in 2007, growing to over 110 acres, which they sell to Ridgeview. Ridgeview, in turn, makes Tinwood's wines – all of which are single vineyard and single vintage – allowing them to invest in growing great fruit and establishing their cellar door and tourism offering, managed by Art's wife Jodie, who is also in charge of their bees and the estate honey.

First to open was the tasting room in 2012, to showcase their maiden vintage, followed by tours, the first three vineyard lodges and a new kitchen and restaurant extension, with the restaurant opening in 2022. A couple of years later five more lodges were built, bringing the total to eight, and each (rather romantic) lodge has a private, slightly raised south-west-facing terrace that overlooks the vines with sunset views at night. Bliss.

The Wines

Only single-estate, single-vintage sparkling wines are made, with their Blanc de Blancs making up around 40 per cent of production.

BRUT VINTAGE
red apple, savoury, brioche, raspberry **£££**

ROSÉ VINTAGE
restrained, red berries, cherry stones **£££**

BLANC DE BLANCS VINTAGE*
elegant, green apple, almond croissant **£££**

Tours & tastings

Open daily (apart from Christmas Day, Boxing Day and New Year's Day), offering coffee, a deli and self-guided wine flights. Relaxed, informal tours run throughout the week, more at weekends. Food pairings can be purchased additionally from the Vineyard Kitchen on the day, with Bronze, Silver and Gold tapas-style sharing boards available. Various events held throughout the year, from DJ parties to an open-air cinema.

Eating

The Vineyard Kitchen's menu changes every three months. Relaxed atmosphere, bifold doors to the terrace, no tablecloths, family-friendly. Weekly afternoon teas and an epic Sunday lunch on big sharing platters.

Good to know

Each lodge is individually and tastefully decorated, with wildflowers on the roof. A three-course dinner hamper (for two) can be delivered to the lodge for the ultimate in privacy, and a breakfast hamper is included. Dogs are welcome (they have two Labs themselves, called Bubbles and Fizz). There is free use of mountain bikes, the sauna and the barrel sauna for lodges 1 to 3.

Wiston Estate

A superlative West Sussex experience, with destination dining

The Wiston story starts many, many years ago, when, in 1743, Elizabeth Fagge of Wiston House married her neighbour, Sir Charles Matthew Goring, thus uniting house, name and land. Whilst death duties in the 1920s resulted in the family having to leave Wiston House to lease it out – it's currently occupied by the Foreign Office – the wider estate has been in the family ever since. Perhaps it is for this reason that they are such sympathetic custodians of the land, setting aside 165 acres as part of the Steyning Downland Scheme and being actively involved in a new nature-restoration initiative called Weald to Waves, a nature corridor with Wiston right at the heart of it.

Today it is Richard and Kirsty who are overseeing this spectacular South Downs spot, having taken over the reins from Richard's parents, Harry and Pip, with Richard's South African-born mother being the driving force behind planting vines at Wiston. On moving to England with her new husband in 1972, Pip missed the vines at home in Franschhoek, which were established by her French Huguenot ancestors, and whilst it might have taken a bit of time and persuasion, her dream and vision to make wine at Wiston came to fruition at last. After some fairly serious interest in their land from a couple of Champagne houses, Harry was finally convinced that it was a great place to plant, and the first vines went in in 2006 – the classic three Champagne varieties – on sixteen acres of south-facing chalk slopes. Twenty years later, over thirty acres are under vine.

What happened next, though, I suspect, was entirely unexpected and something of a coup. Winemaking legend Dermot Sugrue left Nyetimber to come and work at Wiston in 2007, as he was so struck by the potential of the site, famously setting up the winery (with very little budget after planting) in an old turkey abattoir at North Farm. From the outset, however, the quality of the wines was never in doubt; Dermot imported an old Coquard press from France to treat the grapes as gently as possible and used subtle French oak on the base blend. Accolades and gongs swiftly followed, from being named Winery of the Year multiple times by WineGB to being selected for state banquets.

But Wiston lacked a 'hub' where they could showcase their award-winning wines, and so the family turned their attention to hospitality. Another thing that Pip had brought over with her from South Africa was the concept of an 'open-door policy', where what is produced on site is also sold and consumed there; they needed to open up the estate and encourage people to come and visit. And do this they have. Chalk Restaurant, named after the vineyard's chalky soils, was opened in late 2021 and, in my opinion, is one of the very best (if not the best) winery restaurant in the country, with a truly integrated grape-to-glass offering.

The Wines

The wines are elegant and accomplished, and whilst Dermot left Wiston in the capable hands of Marcus and Megan Rayner-Ward to set up his own venture, they remain spectacular. The goal is for the wines to express their unique chalk *terroir* and to have the right amount of acidity to enable long periods of ageing. Whilst some (very good) still wines are now being produced along with the sparklers, the fizz remains a favourite.

CUVÉE VINTAGE*
orchard fruits, opulent, savoury **££££**

ROSÉ NV
rosehip, redcurrant, cherry clafoutis **£££**

BLANC DE BLANCS VINTAGE*
apple Danish, nuts, candied peel **££££**

Tours & tastings

Tastings take place in a sleek tasting room, and regular tours run throughout the year, with core offerings being the Wiston Winery Tour & Tasting and the Vintage Tour & Tasting. Summer also sees the popular Sundown Safari, which in winter becomes Top Drawer. The vineyards are open to visitors. Keep an eye out for their grape-picking days, which sell out in minutes!

Eating

No visit is complete without booking a table at Chalk; this truly is a destination restaurant, serving stellar seasonal food. There is also a funky silver coffee truck (the Chalk Express, aka Gladys) by the vines, and in the summer the courtyard (where dogs are allowed) hosts a caravan, which sells wine, cocktails and charcuterie.

Good to know

The Wiston-owned Pump House is a short drive away and comes complete with one double bedroom, a wood-fired hot tub and a complimentary bottle of bubbles. There are also a host of other wineries to visit locally, including Ambriel Sparkling, Kinsbrook, Nutbourne, Nyetimber, Titch Hill and Digby Fine English in Arundel.

Surrey

Albury Organic Vineyard

The vinous rambler's retreat with wildlife walk

This small, family-run business was set up by Nick Wenman in 2009 – the culmination of a forty-year aspiration – which now sees him working alongside daughter Lucy. They are passionate advocates of sustainability; founding members with Gold certification from the SWGB initiative, as well as practising both organic and biodynamic viticulture.

Albury only use their own organic grapes – predominantly Chardonnay, Pinot Noir and Pinot Meunier, with some Pinot Noir Précoce – in their wines and have a certified biodynamic vineyard that requires special preparations, yeasts and sprays. Their commitment to sustainability has also seen them create an exceptional wildlife walk (open to guests in high season with a donation to the Surrey Wildlife Trust) around the edge of the vineyard, which includes an insect highway, wildflower meadows, bug hotels and an enormous bench shaped like a cow horn, crafted by artist Tom Nicholson-Smith. Situated in an Area of Outstanding Natural Beauty on the North Downs Way in the village of Shere – famously known as being the 'chocolate box' village that features in the 2006 film *The Holiday* – Albury are also located on a popular walking route and footpath.

The very first wine that they made – the delightfully aromatic Silent Pool Rosé (a blend of Pinot Meunier and Pinot Noir grapes) – was served on the Royal Barge to celebrate the Queen's Diamond Jubilee, and routinely sells out very fast. Their sparkling wines are elegant, lightly floral and with pleasing freshness. Also look out for their vermouths and barrel-aged Negroni.

The Wines

Wines are made for them at Litmus Wines, and are both sparkling and still.

CLASSIC CUVÉE VINTAGE honeysuckle, green apple, oatmeal	**£££**
BLANC DE BLANCS VINTAGE light, lemon, apple, biscuit	**£££**
SILENT POOL ROSÉ VINTAGE+ aromatic, sweet shop, orange, strawberry	**££**

Tours & tastings

Weekends only. Self-guided tours and wine flights. Guided tours run May to September. Wine and cheese tastings. Cellar door and shop. Hen-do packages; corporate and private bookings. Events such as willow weaving and Sip & Paint, Kids' Easter Trail, musical events and wildlife adventures. Vineyard Tour & Wildlife Walk. Bee-keeping demonstration. Wine club.

Eating

Local cheese and charcuterie boards and snacks.

Good to know

Dog-friendly: 'walkies and wine' and even a dog menu. If coming by car, don't park at the first car park, but head up the lane. Silent Pool is next door for gin lovers. Perfect Pairings combine the two. Chilworth Manor, Denbies and Greyfriars are all nearby.

Chilworth Manor

A unique spot full of history

If the walls could talk, I suspect Chilworth Manor would have quite a lot to say! From being recorded as a Saxon manor in the Domesday Book, it was then gifted by William the Conqueror to the Bishop of Bayeux, his half-brother, who turned it into a monastery. Situated on the Pilgrims' Way, the monastery's position allowed monks to minister to those travelling to Canterbury at Grade II-listed church St Martha's-on-the-Hill, which is located above the house. Sadly, the alleged secret tunnels linking the two buildings have never been found.

From monks to Sarah Churchill, the Duchess of Marlborough, today the manor is owned by Graham and Mia Wrigley, who purchased Chilworth in 2006. Adjacent to the property was some land that was being used as a paddock, and the Wrigleys found themselves wondering if it would be a good site for vines. So they employed the services of expert Stephen Skelton MW to find out, and he confirmed that the paddock was indeed well situated for viticulture. Given this green light, they set about buying it.

Ten acres of vines were planted on chalky soils – part of the Hythe Formation – in 2013 to the classic varietals of Chardonnay, Pinot Noir and Pinot Meunier, roughly a third of each. A cellar door was also built and the Watch House tasting barn was finished in spring 2024 and is extremely stylish, blending harmoniously into the natural landscape with breathtaking views from the roof. Inside has an equally sympathetic aesthetic, being light, bright and airy, and is the ideal place in which to relax and taste their outstanding wines.

A still Provençal-style rosé is made and, rather fun, a glögg in reference to Mia's Swedish roots, but the real stars of the show are the sparkling wines, which impress enormously. Lees ageing is on the longer side (five years for the Alwyn) and the balance of freshness coupled with complex yeasty notes is almost unparalleled. The sparkling rosé is amongst the best I have tasted, and the prices for wines of this quality are competitive; after enjoying a glass you might be in danger of never wanting to leave.

The Wines

Single-estate, single-vintage wines are made by Matthieu Elzinga.

CLASSIC CUVÉE ALWYN VINTAGE
nuts, spice, toast, brioche, croissant — **£££**

BRUT ROSÉ VINTAGE*
red fruits, fruit tart, cherry Bakewell — **£££**

ROSÉ VINTAGE+
subtle, cranberry, raspberry pip, lemon — **££**

Tours & tastings

Select dates throughout the year. Friday Night Fizz takes place once a month during spring and summer. Word and Wine; Bob Geldof spoke at one. Private tours. Chilworth Wine Festival runs annually in early summer, as does charity event Picnics and Pinks.

Eating

Afternoon tea and sparkling wine. Caterers available for private or corporate events.

Good to know

Members' club. When the cellar door is open, guests can walk Winston's Trail, named after their old dog. Founding member of the SWGB. Plenty of walking trails nearby.

Denbies Wine Estate

The original visitor offering in Box Hill

Whilst I'd never previously heard of Denbies being dubbed the 'Disney of Wine', when I was told that it had been, I could certainly understand why, given the sheer scale of their offering. Originally, wines were sold out of a barn, but in 1993 a visitor centre was built to show guests how wine is made, from vine to glass. A small train and people mover would take visitors to the winery, a little cinema and the cellar for a tasting, and that ran for around twenty years before moving to an outdoor train, which has allowed guests to be taken up the track and around the vineyard to enjoy the whole estate and its incomparable views.

It's a far cry from when Adrian White bought the 630-acre estate pig and cattle farm – named after sixteenth-century farmer John Denby – in 1986. Geologist Professor Richard Selley recommended planting vines on the south-facing chalk slopes and so in went a wide selection of varieties, which today includes Chardonnay, Pinot Noir, Pinot Meunier, Ortega, Seyval Blanc, Bacchus, Solaris, Müller-Thurgau and Reichensteiner, covering some 265 acres of the North Downs. Denbies is still family owned, and run by Adrian's son, Chris, who has been steering the ship for some twenty-five years, with 2026 marking its fortieth anniversary.

Sustainability is important here; they have B Corp certification, won a King's Award for Enterprise for Sustainable Development, and the vineyards and winery are certified net zero. The vineyard sheep, woodland, bat boxes, beehives and wildflower meadows can be seen whilst enjoying the grounds of this impressive, pioneering estate, with some 400,000 visitors a year doing just that.

The Wines

A broad range of almost twenty wines are made by chief winemaker John Worontschak and cellar master Andy Kershaw.

CUBITT BLANC DE BLANCS VINTAGE* apple crumble, savoury, saline, attractive	£££
ORANGE SOLARIS VINTAGE+* grippy, bitter orange, kumquat, dried apricot	£
SURREY GOLD NV+ lightly floral, citrus, jasmine, melon, honeysuckle	£

Tours & tastings

Two trains run on the weekends. Tours run all year round: sparkling afternoon train tour, indoor winery wine-tasting tour, the Secret Vineyard two-hour walking trail, private tours. Hen-dos welcome. Weddings, private events, corporate events. Loyalty club.

Eating

Fine dining with 360-degree views at the Gallery Restaurant in the Tower. Brunch, food and wine matching, sparkling afternoon tea and dinner are offered at the hotel's superior Vineyard Restaurant and Wine Library. Fondue at the two cabanas. Takeaway food from the Hatch, and the Conservatory serves hot food, scones and refreshments.

Good to know

On-site accommodation at the carbon-neutral Vineyard Hotel (there are two separate areas: the Farmhouse and the Brokes, and dogs are welcome at the latter). Farm shop. Bacchus Half Marathon and 10k every September.

Greyfriars Vineyard

A relaxed day out in the Surrey Hills

Vets Phil and Bill originally planted a hobby vineyard with 1.5 acres of Chardonnay and Pinot Noir, on their own rootstocks, in 1989, with current owners Mike and Hilary Wagstaff extending plantings to around forty acres. On leaving corporate life, Mike Wagstaff found himself in a bit of a conundrum: too young to fully retire, but he hated golf, so what to do? Fortuitously, the purchase of the 'house of their dreams' brought him and wife Hilary to the area, and they subsequently ended up, in 2010, being the proud owners of Greyfriars Vineyard just a couple of miles away.

Plantings are now across two sites – both have south-facing chalky slopes – with Pinot Meunier being added. Around 90 per cent of plantings are made up of the classic three varieties, along with Pinot Blanc, Pinot Gris and Sauvignon Blanc. The goal was always to become a boutique but commercial producer of predominantly sparkling wines, with Mike initially making them himself. Proudly English, they never sought to mimic Champagne, wanting to showcase their own unique *terroir* instead.

In 2018 they decided that one of the best ways of doing that was by going 'direct to consumer', but on setting up a website, they noticed that around 90 per cent of traffic was actually looking for tours and experiences rather than buying wine. So they started with a limited, rather weather-dependent tour offering and a tiny shop (the old cattle shed), but could very much see that demand was there.

This then exploded during the pandemic with people wanting staycations, experiences and to connect with their food and wine, and so over lockdown they built their tasting room, complete with a 194-wineglass chandelier by John the Blacksmith, to enable them to offer a year-round experience. Opening in 2021, this transformed their ability to offer events to a wide demographic of wine lovers seeking to spend a day in the vines.

The Wines

They want to 'provide great wines at accessible prices' and they certainly do.

SAUVIGNON BLANC VINTAGE+
subtle, lemon, grapefruit, tangy **£**

OLD VINES BLANC DE BLANCS VINTAGE*
lemon, nuts, spice, toast, long **£££**

ROSÉ RESERVE VINTAGE
pale, rose petals, strawberries and cream **££**

Tours & tastings

The tasting room and cellar door are open all year round. Good-value tours with al fresco tasting. Predominantly high season, weekends only. Horsebox bar in the vineyards by the decking. Off-season tours after harvest until December. Seasonal events: yoga and wine, pasta-making, wreath-making, sip and paint, cheese and wine. Private and corporate bookings. Wine club.

Eating

Pop-up food trucks some weekends, high season only. BYO picnic for Bottle and Blanket by the vineyard: pay corkage and blanket hire.

Good to know

Albury and Chilworth Manor are twenty minutes away.

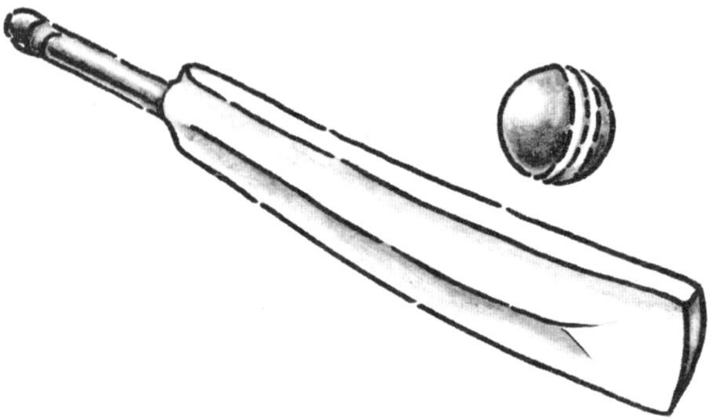

Hampshire

Black Chalk

The old dairy farm now making classic English sparklers

After a number of inspirational vinous encounters whilst travelling, Jacob Leadley enrolled at Plumpton College and then left his job in London to become a winemaker, initially at Hattingley, before setting up Black Chalk with some of his family. At first, grapes were bought in from local vineyards, with the wines being made at nearby Cottonworth – their first vintage was 2015, with the wine being released in 2018. From those modest beginnings, they now have thirty acres under vine: ten at Rivers Vineyard with the remaining twenty split equally across two others (Hide and the Levels), all on chalk soils. Plantings are mainly Chardonnay, Pinot Noir and Pinot Meunier, with some Pinot Gris and Pinot Noir Précoce. Fruit is only from their own vineyards, with the exception of the Chardonnay for their still wine, which is from Kit's Coty in Kent.

In 2020 Black Chalk found the ideal site for their winery, hidden in the Test Valley: an old dairy farm with dilapidated buildings that they transformed not just into a winery but also a tasting room, an outside courtyard and the Loft, an event space. In terms of their wine style, they take a 'base-led approach to the wine'. They have some thirty-four different clone and rootstock combinations, which are all handled separately, favouring a fruit-forward style of wine with an acidic backbone, which means 90 per cent of the wines are fermented in stainless steel, with a tiny bit of old oak for body and texture. Their premium sparkling wines are 'Paragon' and 'Inversion' (a Blanc de Blancs and a Blanc de Noirs).

The transformed buildings of the farm now offer a really attractive hub for visitors, with the tasting room being in the old dairy or milking parlour, which leads out to an attractive courtyard and a path to the distinctive and rather lovely Circle Vineyard, a lawn with picnic benches and tables that is encircled by vines: a very special spot to sit and savour a glass (or two) of Black Chalk vino.

The Wines

Predominantly sparkling wines showcasing zippy, higher acidity styles.

CLASSIC VINTAGE
zesty, fresh, nuts, apples — £££

WILD ROSE VINTAGE
pale, crunchy, cranberry, rosehip — ££££

DANCER IN PINK ROSÉ VINTAGE+*
raspberry, cherry blossom, red apple — ££

RUMOUR HAS IT CHARDONNAY VINTAGE+
sappy, spicy, delicate, fresh — £££

Tours & tastings

Run all year round in high season; spring to late summer, but they also offer winter tours and many come with lunch. Typically run at the weekends. Private tours. Wine club. Tasting room and shop open seven days a week. Pop-up events.

Eating

Boards with local cheeses, charcuterie, smoked fish or paté. Special boards and nibbles. Afternoon tea. Cake. Friday Night Lates run in high season, with different food vendors on rotation.

Good to know

For gin lovers, Bombay Sapphire distillery is around twenty minutes away.

Exton Park Vineyard

Tours, tastings and an impressive event space

At the grand old age of seventy-nine, the late Malcolm Isaac MBE bought Exton Park Vineyard, as he was looking for a 'passion project' after selling his Vitacress Salads business, built up from a mere acre of watercress in 1951. Situated in the South Downs, the sixty-acre single vineyard is planted with Chardonnay, Pinot Noir and Pinot Meunier, and at first, the grapes were sold to Hampshire producer Coates & Seely.

But a winery was finished in 2011, and acclaimed winemaker Corinne Seely joined the team, having previously worked at Domaine de Chevalier and around the world. Whilst many producers focus on vintage wines, Exton Park always concentrated on building up a library of reserve wines so that they could consistently blend between vintages and showcase additional complexity from these older wines. The 'RB' on the non-vintage labels stands for Reserve Blend and the number next to it reflects the amount of different reserve wines that went into the specific wine: thirty-two for RB|32, twenty-eight for the Blanc de Noirs and twenty-three for the rosé. The most is forty-five for the Blanc de Blancs. Long lees ageing is also utilised across the range, with three years minimum being the norm. A small selection of vintage wines are also made and, unusually, they experiment with sea ageing – which provides dark, cool and consistent conditions – too. A duo of wines can be purchased – the 60 Above and 60 Below Prestige Pack – to compare the difference between cellar and sea ageing.

Wines are, understandably, highly regarded at this prestigious producer and although Malcolm passed away in 2024, it was not before he had realised his dream, leaving this stunning legacy behind.

The Wines

Made by well-regarded French winemaker Corinne Seely.

RB|32 BRUT*
honeysuckle, marzipan, nuts, citrus, tarte tatin, complex **£££**

RB|28 BLANC DE NOIRS
red fruits, raspberry, spice, cherry, plum **££££**

RB|23 ROSÉ
pale colour, crunchy, cherry blossom, rosehip **£££**

PINOT MEUNIER ROSÉ VINTAGE
rose gold, orange blossom, quince, plum **£££££**

Tours & tastings

Tours run on Friday mornings all year round. Small groups only. Private tastings. Corporate events: Exton Hall is typically hired for exclusive use, though other spaces can be booked separately; they have a boardroom, the Great Hall, a downstairs tasting room, a club room, a Mezzanine bar and a dining room complete with a chef's table.

Eating

An in-house chef is available for functions and events.

Good to know

Hambledon Wine Estate is only fifteen minutes away and Raimes English Sparkling less than twenty.

Hambledon Vineyard

A swoon-worthy setup in the birthplace of English wine

With not one but two noteworthy accolades to their name, one could almost accuse Hambledon of being greedy! Not only are they based in the village of the same name, which is the home or 'cradle' of cricket, but they are also widely regarded as being the first modern, commercial winery. Original owner, forward-thinking Major-General Sir Guy Salisbury-Jones planted vines here in 1952, and on his death Mill Down House and the vineyard were sold, changing hands again in 1999, when it was bought by biochemist, banker and wine lover Ian Kellett, who took himself off to Plumpton College to learn more about it.

Planning to make sparkling wines, in 2002 he planted ten acres of the classic French varieties Chardonnay, Pinot Noir and Pinot Meunier on Newhaven chalk soils – the same chalk that runs under the Channel from Champagne to Hampshire – using a wide variety of different Burgundian clones and rootstock combinations to see qualitatively which would work best. A winery followed, along with further vineyard expansion – some 200 acres – and huge (over) investment in a visitor offering.

The property was subsequently sold in September 2023 to Berry Bros & Rudd and Symington Family Estates, with winemaking overseen by Hervé Jestin and Felix Gabillet. Style-wise the wines are very much '*terroir* driven', so that the Hampshire chalk soils can shine through, bringing freshness, elegance, a linear structure and minerality. They are also non-vintage, gravity fed, favour minimal intervention, low dosage, and use around 20–25 per cent reserve wines. The resulting range is rather ravishing, with the entry-level Classic Cuvée being a real standout (I popped one in my trolley this very week!), but all are united by impressive lengths and sheer drinkability.

Alongside the wines is a breathtaking visitor centre and restaurant, which are not to be missed. The cellar door (the door of which is festooned with beautiful ferns and foliage) is full of vinous temptations, before leading upstairs to the all-wood bar and restaurant – even wooden dowels are used in lieu of screws – along with private dining and tasting rooms. This is a truly spectacular space and one I'd wholeheartedly recommend visiting; if I could pick it up and move it closer to my house, I would. Lush.

The Wines

Wines are non-vintage and head winemaker Hervé Jestin is ex-Champagne Duval-Leroy.

CLASSIC CUVÉE NV*
complex, nuts, citrus, sourdough, apple — ££££

CLASSIC CUVÉE ROSÉ NV
pale, raspberry, red apples, berries — ££££

PREMIÈRE CUVÉE NV
hazelnuts, apples, lemon peel, refined — £££££

BLANC DE BLANCS CUVÉE NV
fresh, poised, biscuit, apple Danish — £££££

Tours & tastings

Run all year round. Estate Tour & Tasting in spring and summer with a winter option outside this. Guided Tasting Flight of four wines. The Winemaker's Insight Tour & Tasting and a luxury Grenadier Vineyard Safari Tour & Tasting for four people. Pop-up events include Father's Day Fayre, Jazz & Fizz, Harvest Party. Three tier wine club. WSET Level 1 & 2 provider. Cellar-door shop with gifts and a great range of wines, including Berry Bros bottles.

Eating

The roomy Michelin Guide-recommended restaurant offers an 'informal but fine-dining experience' with no double bookings, so diners don't feel rushed. Wraparound balcony and terrace. Seasonal food. Set menu or à la carte and seasonal menus; for example, Harvest Lunch. Kids' menu. Dog-friendly. Pizza oven and sharing plates in the courtyard in the summer, walk-ins only. Guest chef evenings. Private dining.

Good to know

Plenty of cycle routes and walking paths nearby, with a bike park on site.

Hattingley Valley

The award-winning winery with assemblage at its core

Upon semi-retiring, Simon Robinson bought a farm but wanted to diversify from arable farming, cattle and sheep into grape growing, inspired in part by the success of Nyetimber, but also the greater shelf life and export potential of wine versus his cows or crops! Decision made, he planted the first vines at Hattingley – named after the small hamlet – in 2008 putting in Chardonnay, Pinot Noir and Pinot Meunier with the singular aim of producing sparkling wines.

The first vineyard site to be planted was Chalky Hill and then the aptly named New Site in 2011, bringing the total number of plantings to twenty-two acres. Wines are made partly from Hattingley Valley's own fruit, but they also work with long-term growers in Kent, Sussex, Suffolk and Hampshire, which they feel helps to mitigate against potential regional weather issues. Knowing very little about winemaking, Simon employed superstar winemaker Emma Rice to help establish both the eco-friendly, bells and whistles, 450-tonne winery and their wine style.

From the very beginning their style encapsulated balance – fruit, acidity and mousse – ease of drinking and approachability, with the use of oak being their 'quiet signature'. Oak softens acidity and adds a creamy texture; they use only French barrels – almost all old – and roughly 10–15 per cent of the base blend will see oak for around six months, with more for the prestige cuvées. Head winemaker Rob McCulloch, who took over from Emma in 2022, explains that they also use 'a range of fermentation techniques' such as partial MLF, wild ferments, barrel fermentations and reserve wines to create layers of complexity; there may be as many as 40 different components in their Classic Reserve. As such, there is a firm understanding of the importance of blending or *assemblage*, coupled with 'believing very strongly in long lees ageing'. Ultimately, they are looking to create 'classic' wines that aren't copying Champagne but that are delicious and uniquely English.

On the labels of these wines is a beautiful butterfly motif that adorns the range. It is also hidden inside the foil, found only when you open a bottle, chosen because silver-washed fritillary butterflies were found on their original Chalky Hill site, reflecting the healthy biodiversity of the vineyard, which is SWGB-certified.

The Wines

Wines are made by friend and fellow MW Rob McCulloch.

CLASSIC RESERVE NV
citrus, apple, nutty, spiced oats **£££**

BLANC DE BLANCS VINTAGE*
delicate, spice, lemon peel, brioche **£££££**

ROSÉ VINTAGE
ballerina pink, raspberry, strawberry, citrus **£££**

ENTICE BACCHUS DESSERT WINE (HALF BOTTLE)+
floral, perfumed, pear, stone fruits **££**

Tours & tastings
Weekends in low season, and additional days in high season (mid-spring to pre-harvest). Private tours.

Eating
Nothing on site but plenty in nearby New Alresford.

Good to know
The Grange, Raimes Sparkling and Black Chalk are nearby.

Raimes English Sparkling

Enjoy sparkling wines in an enchanting setting

The fifteen acres of vines on this single estate are part of an enormous 1,800-acre family farm, with Augusta Raimes being the fifth generation to work it but the first to grow vines. These were first planted in 2011, with about ten acres of Chardonnay, Pinot Noir and Pinot Meunier on south-facing, chalk and flint soils. Further plantings went in around ten years later, with vines now found in three different but adjacent fields.

There are five wines in the range – all of which are vintage – with a demi-sec (made from 100 per cent Chardonnay) also produced, as well as the wines listed. Lees ageing is long – at least three years – and dosage tends to be fairly low. The Blanc de Noirs is a standout: distinctive, serious and well crafted, with the 2013 vintage being their very first release.

The award-winning sparkling wines – no still wines are made – can be tasted in the attractive Tasting Barn (only opened in 2023, and which used to be a farmyard overlooked by horses), either on the ground or first floor. It's light and airy but with cosy alpine vibes; there is a long central table both upstairs and down, with smaller ones scattered around. Large windows allow for expansive vine views, and wooden boxes offer plenty of blankets for sitting outside in the summer when it starts to get chilly. A small kitchen prepares delicious food.

The Wines

Wines are made at nearby Hattingley Valley.

CLASSIC VINTAGE
nuts, apple tart, apple blossom, citrus — **£££**

BLANC DE BLANCS VINTAGE
subtle, lemon posset, cashews, meringue — **££££**

BLANC DE NOIRS VINTAGE*
honeycomb, spice, nuts, toffee apple — **£££**

ROSÉ VINTAGE
delicate, cherry blossom, pink grapefruit, frangipane — **££££**

Tours & tastings

The Tasting Barn and cellar door is open from Easter until the end of December. Vineyard tours run from spring to late summer, with the cellar door open at weekends. Walk-ins welcome for self-guided wine flights. Guided flights. Private tours. Corporate events.

Eating

Bar nibbles, cheese and charcuterie boards. Weekend Sparkling Cream Tea.

Good to know

Plenty of other wineries to visit within a half-hour radius, including The Grange, Exton Park, Hattingley, Hambledon and Black Chalk. Dogs and children welcome.

The Grange

Small group tours near this historic Hampshire estate

The Baring banking family arguably needs little introduction, but over 200 years ago, Alexander Baring bought The Grange Estate, which included a nineteenth-century neoclassical house. Today the house is empty and was gifted to English Heritage on a long lease, but the wider estate and land is still owned by the family, which includes siblings Mark, Zam, Rose and Lucy.

It is good-natured Zam who manages the vineyard and winery, owned equally by the four siblings, who set it up in 2011 after careers in finance, television, publishing and design respectively. Established on the edge of the family farm, the classic three varietals of Chardonnay, Pinot Noir and Pinot Meunier were planted (a third of each) on twenty-five acres of the Burges Farm vineyard, which is south-facing, with loam soils over chalk. Despite having considered using the land for rearing organic lamb or producing rapeseed oil, it was ultimately decided that they would produce sparkling wine as the site was so suitable.

At the start they sold their grapes to Hattingley Valley but then started making their own wines there with consultant Emma Rice, before building a winery in 2022 and employing ex-Gusbourne winemaker Harry Pickering. Four sparkling wines are produced, including an elegant Blanc de Blancs and two still wines – a moreish Chardonnay and a dry rosé.

The Wines

The Grange are proponents of long lees ageing and time on cork for additional complexity.

THE CLASSIC NV almond croissant, nutty, savoury	£££
THE PINK NV pale, crunchy, restrained, raspberry, rosehip	££££
THE WHITE FROM BLACK VINTAGE red cherries, redcurrant, nuts	££££

Tours & tastings

Around eighteen small group tours are hosted annually, about three a month from mid-spring; weekends only. Private tours. Corporate events. Weddings. Pop-up Christmas market. Gift vouchers. First Pressings wine club membership.

Eating

Nothing on site but options locally.

Good to know

Plenty of accommodation in the wider estate, including The Clocktower, Garden Cottage and the larger Farm House and Lake House Cottage. Ring the cellar-door/tasting-room doorbell during office hours (including Saturday morning) to buy wine. Close to Hattingley and Raimes Sparkling, with Black Chalk, Exton Park and Bluestone around thirty minutes away. Dogs and children welcome. The Grange Festival – an opera and arts festival – is hosted annually at the house.

Berkshire

Stanlake Park Wine Estate

Beautiful grounds a short hop from the Elizabeth Line

The exquisite sixteenth-century walled garden here houses the oldest Gewürztraminer in the country, part of the 500 'pilot' vines that owner Jon Leighton planted in 1979, when he set up Thames Valley Vineyard, before selling it in 2005 when he moved to Australia. Amazingly, a lot of those original vines still remain – now some of the oldest vines in England – and are a mix of heritage varieties such as Optima and Dornfelder, and French ones like Pinot Noir. Hybrids and PIWIs such as Solaris and Muscaris are also planted, and in total about ten acres of the 130-acre estate are under vine, with soils mostly being loam with clay and sand. Stanlake Park only use their own fruit for the wines.

The current owner inherited the vineyard and winery when he bought the estate in 2013, which dates back to 1166 and used to be part of Windsor Great Park, but decided to keep it on, employing winemaker Nico Centonze and his partner Natalia Pezzone – who has been instrumental in driving hospitality – to help manage it. The winery is housed in a Grade II-listed building, the Reformation Barn, and a wide range of wines are made here: five fizzes (bottled using more traditional labels) and some ten still wines displaying attractive, floral designs. The wines are made from an eclectic blend of Germanic varietals such as Seyval Blanc, Bacchus and Dornfelder (the Regatta uses Optima, Reichensteiner, Gewürztraminer and Schönburger) but also classic French, providing a range of styles and price points. The garden makes a truly bucolic spot in which to sit back, relax and enjoy a sparkling Bacchus Brut.

The Wines

Nico makes fresh, modern, well-made, affordable wines.

BACCHUS BRUT NV*
fresh, pear, floral, pineapple, fun — ££

STANLAKE BRUT NV
red apples, apple Danish, nuts — ££

BACCHUS VINTAGE+
restrained, citrus, peas — £

ORANGE VINTAGE+
quince, jasmine, orange zest — £

PINOT NOIR ROSÉ VINTAGE+
strawberry, raspberry, rosehip — £

Tours & tastings

Classic Wine Tour & Tasting or the Wine & Cheese Tour. Wine & Cheese Tasting. Walk-in Tasting Flights. Sauna & Sip. Pilates. Charlotte Tilbury make-up events. WSET provider. Private tours. Corporate events. Weddings. Cellar shop. Private hire of the Tasting Shed and Wine Bar out of hours.

Eating

Food served from the Wine Bar: nibbles, snacks and deli boards (cheese and charcuterie with vegan option). Cream teas.

Good to know

North Lodge Cottage (sleeps two) and South Lodge (sleeps eight). An additional eight rooms are being built. Dog-friendly on site. Oaken Grove Vineyard, Hundred Hills, Jojo's Vineyard and Harrow & Hope are all within a thirty-minute drive.

Oxfordshire

Hundred Hills

The members'-club model in the Chilterns

The name Hundred Hills stems from the winery being located in the ancient Pyrton Hundred; a hundred being a term that relates to being able to raise one hundred men from a specific hilly area, smaller than a county, to fight. This decidedly hilly area was finally found by Stephen and Fiona Duckett in 2012 after a three-year search, using the expertise of the late Dr Michel Salgues, a former chef du cave at Roederer Estate, who helped establish the Anderson Valley winery in the United States before becoming a wine consultant.

Whilst the search started in Kent and Sussex, they eventually found the steep chalky slopes of what was to become their vineyard in the Stoner Valley of the Chilterns. Planting started in 2014 and there are forty-two acres under vine, planted with Burgundian clones of Chardonnay and Pinot Noir over six different parcels: Hill Top, the Amphitheatre, Meadow Woods, the Winery Bank (1 & 2) and Hillside.

The Wines

All single-estate, sparkling wines made by owner Stephen Duckett, who was trained by Michel.

FIRST EDITION MAGNUM VINTAGE*
hazelnuts, crumble, spiced oats, pastry £££££

BLANC DE BLANCS LIBRARY RELEASE VINTAGE
elegant, linear, lemon meringue, nuts £££££

Tours & tastings

You can only visit if you are a Friend of Hundred Hills, their members' club. Annual fee, paid in two instalments, but you get wine delivered to that value twice a year. No joining fee and membership can be cancelled at any time. Benefit from cellar-door prices with a decent discount if you visit in person. Access to the magnum cellar, tastings and complimentary invitations to seasonal events.

Eating

Nothing on site.

Good to know

Sub-label Doe Eyed Queen, a vegan sparkling wine with a slightly higher dosage, founded by their daughter Amy, is also made here. JoJo's Vineyard is under ten minutes away, with Harrow & Hope and Stanlake Park being accessible within half an hour.

South West

An absolute delight to visit, the South West mixes coastal cool with rural escapes and 'vibey' towns such as Frome and Bruton. Wine-wise there is a wide selection to choose from made by second generation winemakers, farming families who have recently diversified into viticulture and luxury boutique hotels with vineyards. There is plenty to taste, discover and explore here in these holiday hot spots with some stand-out wines.

1. Three Choirs Vineyards
2. Woodchester Valley
3. Carvers Hill Estate
4. Furleigh Estate
5. Langham Wine Estate
6. Saddle Goose
7. Wraxall Vineyard
8. Lyme Bay Winery
9. Lympstone Manor Hotel
10. Sandridge Barton
11. Camel Valley
12. Trevibban Mill

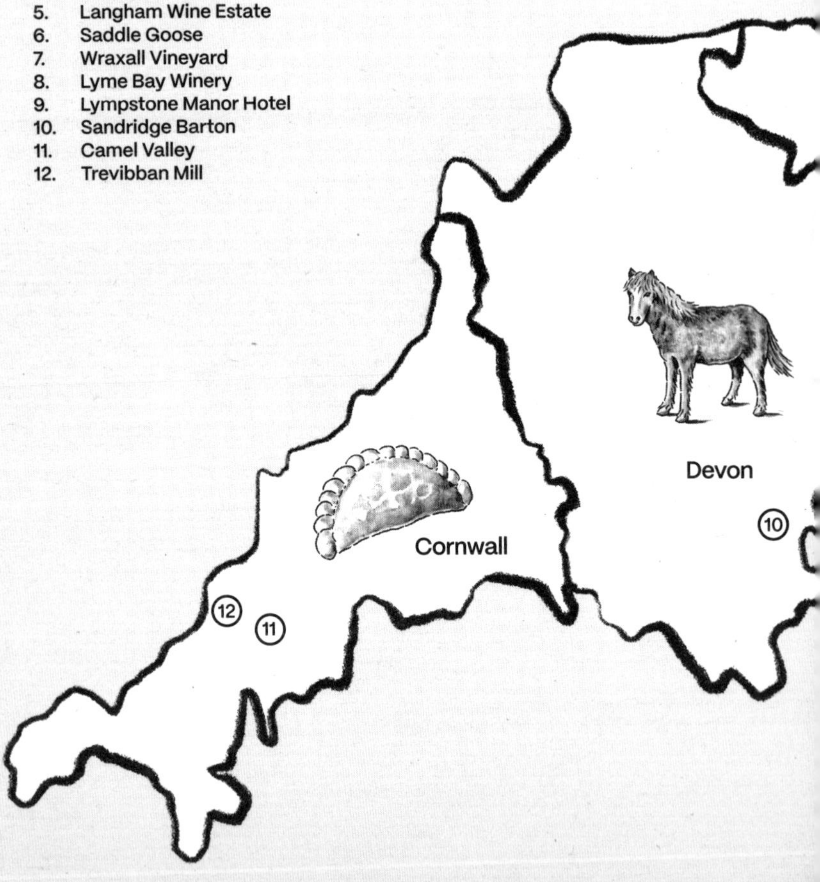

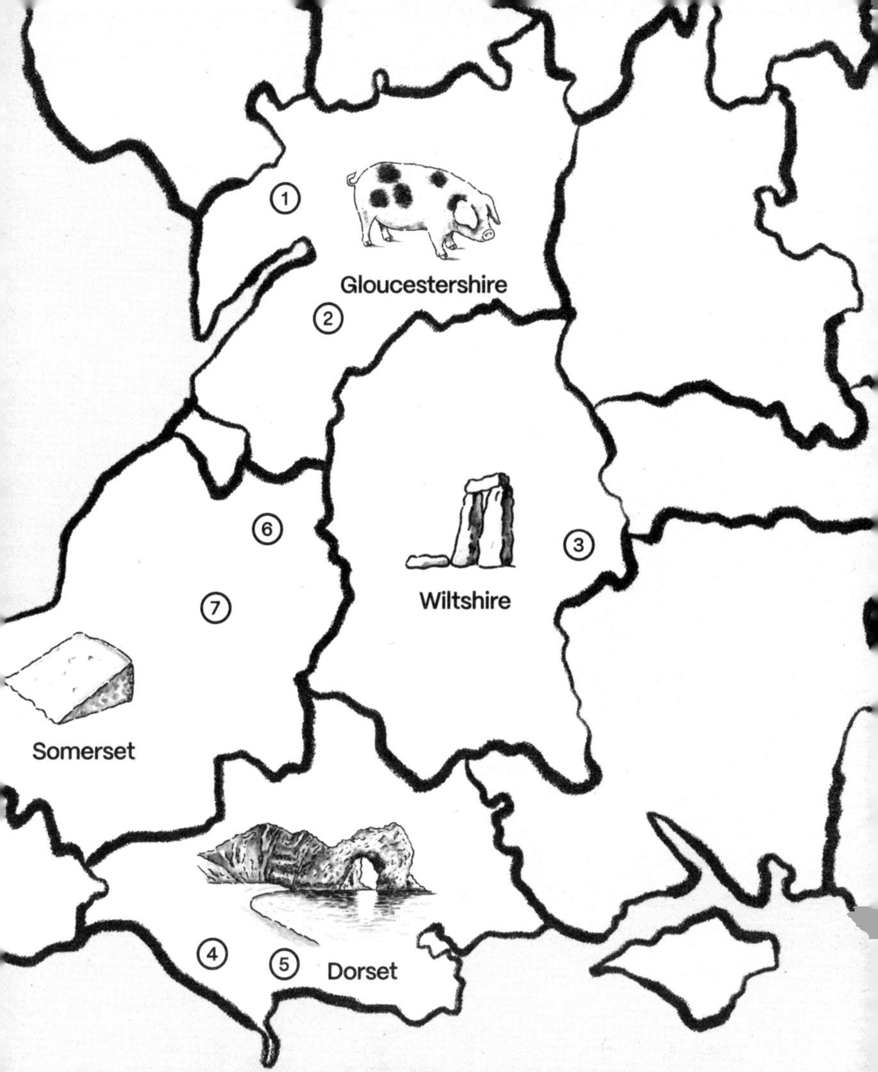

1
Gloucestershire
2
6
3
Wiltshire
7
Somerset
4
5
Dorset

Gloucestershire

Three Choirs Vineyards

One of England's oldest vineyards

Alan McKechnie started Three Choirs, or Fairfield Fruit Farm as it was known then, in 1973, making it one of the oldest vineyards in England. Sadly, he had to sell it eleven years later due to poor health, but it was bought and run by John Oldacre until he died in 2001, though it is still largely owned by the Oldacre family to this day. Under their guardianship it has grown to seventy-five acres of predominantly heritage varieties, of which there are now fourteen, including Bacchus and Siegerrebe, grown on sandy loam soils.

It was John who changed the name to Three Choirs Vineyard, inspired by the Three Choirs Festival, an annual choral event spanning Gloucester, Hereford and Worcester, with the vineyard being relatively close to all three cities. In this second iteration, a new winery was opened, overseen by winemaker Martin Fowkes, who has worked at Three Choirs for over forty years, starting in the vineyards alongside Tom Day, who was to become his father-in-law. Wines are largely still – there are only a couple of sparkling wines – and made from the aforementioned heritage varieties, including off-dry, dry white and rosé blends, along with a single varietal Bacchus. Ravens Hill is a blend of Regent, Rondo and Pinot Noir. Only the sparkling Pinot Noir rosé and Pinot Noir Précoce red are made exclusively from French varietals.

The Wines

Good-value, easy-drinking wines boasting Germanic grapes.

CLASSIC CUVÉE NV
floral, honeysuckle, pear, lemon meringue ££

WILLOW BROOK VINTAGE+
off-dry, juicy, rose, pineapple, stone fruits £

RAVENS HILL VINTAGE+*
damsons, cherries, spice, cherry chocolate £

Tours & tastings

Various options, including weekend self-guided wine tasting with lunch and vineyard walk; guided winery tour, tasting and lunch (spring through to autumn), and separate tours and tastings for residents. Or order a paddle of five wines with food chosen separately.

Eating

The brasserie serves small plates and tapas.

Good to know

Eight Deluxe Vineyard View rooms or three Luxury Lodges with gorgeous verandas. Dogs allowed in the restaurant.

Woodchester Valley

The South Cotswolds winery with chic accommodation

Inspired by the history of Roman viticulture in the area, five years after Fiona Shiner and her husband Neil returned to Gloucestershire – where they had both grown up – they set up Woodchester Valley, close to their family home in Amberley. First planted to just a single acre of Bacchus, with the wines initially being made at Three Choirs, there are now fifty-eight acres under vine, and they also have their own winery (built in 2016) and winemaker.

Wines are a mixture of both still and sparkling, made from grape varieties that include Chardonnay, Pinot Noir and Pinot Meunier, but also Sauvignon Blanc, Seyval Blanc, Pinot Noir Précoce, Regent, Solaris, Ortega, Pinot Gris and Siegerrebe. These varieties are planted over three separate vineyards – Woodchester, Amberley and Stonehouse – in the Stroud (or Five) Valleys, which are largely gently sloping, south, east and south-west facing, with predominantly limestone soils.

There are three sparkling wines in the core range: Cotswold Classic, a Reserve Cuvée and a vintage Rosé Brut, and all wines are single estate; no fruit is bought in. Still wines are very good, with the semi-aromatic whites such as Bacchus and Sauvignon Blanc shining. As well as offering visitor tours and tastings (even dog-friendly ones) there is an impressive range of accommodation on site too with the vineyard barns making the ideal romantic retreat for wine lovers.

The Wines

Affordable, approachable, well-made wines by Jeremy Mount, offering a range of styles.

COTSWOLD CLASSIC NV baked apple, honey, citrus, floral	££
RESERVE CUVÉE NV honeysuckle, lemon, raspberry	£££
ORPHEUS BACCHUS VINTAGE+ grapefruit, citrus, nettles	££
PINOT PRÉCOCE VINTAGE+ spice, plums, cherries, chocolate	££

Tours & tastings

All year round and during the week too. Premium (sparkling emphasis with matched nibbles) or Classic (still) tour and tasting. Tour with picnic lunch. Vineyard dog walk. Geology vineyard tour. Wine club. Harvest festival.

Eating

Grazing lunches available or a fish and chips lunch. There is also a monthly Fizz & Chips supper. Pinot and Pizza.

Good to know

Plentiful accommodation: three beautifully appointed two-person vineyard barns, the Retreat (dog-friendly) that sleeps four to six, and Woodchester Valley House, which sleeps twelve. Their cellar door is at a different site a few minutes away by car, on the Bath Road.

Wiltshire

Carvers Hill Estate

A jaw-dropping new addition to the English wine scene

This enormous, all-singing, all-dancing winery and event space currently makes just the one wine, a still rosé, although some sparkling rosé is being aged on lees for future release and a Chardonnay is also on the way. Around eleven acres of vines have been planted – in 2021 – within the wider 600-acre estate, on greensand soil over chalk with south-east-facing slopes, situated in an area of Outstanding Natural Beauty in the North Wessex Downs. The varieties found here are Chardonnay, Pinot Noir, Pinot Meunier and Pinot Noir Précoce.

The land – Carvers Hill Farm – was bought in 2007 by Tim and Denise Griffiths and is predominantly farmed for arable crops, but Tim saw the potential for viticulture too, having made his first foray into wine when he invested in Domaine de Bellevue in Bordeaux, along with winemaker Jean-François Boras. The pair established an 'exclusive' members' club – Le Grand Société – through which to sell the wines, and the same model has been implemented here.

The only wine at present is the Carvers Hill Estate Primo Rosé vintage (though the aforementioned new sparkling is imminent). The predominantly Pinot Noir – for backbone and structure – and Pinot Noir Précoce – for colour and bouquet – grapes were hand-picked and whole-bunch pressed before being fermented with commercial yeast in stainless-steel tanks, with six months on the lees to add texture, resulting in a dry, tasty, red berry fruited wine.

The Wines

Consultant Emma Rice worked with the team to get the winery established, whilst the winemaker is Patrick Golson.

STILL ROSÉ VINTAGE+
good colour, cherries, strawberries, fresh **££**

Tours & tastings

There is a Guided Tour & Tasting, a Grand Tour and a Sundowner Tour. Private and group tours are also available. A 'vetted' members' club offers exclusive events, and a visitor centre includes private event spaces, a club room for members, a cellar door where wine can be purchased, and a bonded warehouse for fine wine storage.

Eating

Lunch platters are included as part of the Grand Tour.

Good to know

There are three cabins on site: Bluebell, Betony and Sanfoin, and a larger house, Carvers Hill Lodge, is also available to hire. Bluestone is around thirty minutes away.

Dorset

Furleigh Estate

The Dorset winery five miles from the Jurassic Coast

When Rebecca Hansford and her husband Ian Edwards had the opportunity to buy back her childhood home and its eighty-five acres of farmland, they jumped at it. Her family had bought Furleigh at auction in 1954, running it as a dairy farm, before selling it in 1993, but then just over ten years later, it was back on the market, so they made the move from Surrey to Dorset with their three children, keen to pursue something different. They weren't too sure what that was, or what to do with the land, but they had the soils analysed and decided that they were going to establish a vineyard and winery to make wine.

Ian went off to Plumpton College and they planted their first vines. As they were planning on making sparkling wines, they put Chardonnay, Pinot Noir and Pinot Meunier in, as well as Bacchus and Rondo, over two different sites, one being at the farm and the other at their Hingsdon Lane vineyard. They now have around forty acres of vines over the two locations, with both having Thorncombe Sand soils: free-draining, sandy, loamy soils. Although they aren't certified organic, they don't use any pesticides or herbicides, helped by Dorset's relatively mild, sunny climate and long growing season.

The winery was built in 2007, ready for their first commercial harvest two years later. Although they produce a fairly broad range of wines, both still and sparkling, they make slightly more fizz, only using juice from the initial pressing, which goes into stainless steel and has full MLF. They also use reserve wines. Sustainability is important and they have solar panels, reduce waste, and use recycled cardboard and glass. Outside of the land planted to vines, there are wildflower meadows and woodland.

The Wines

Wines are made on site from their own fruit and all are vegan.

CLASSIC CUVÉE VINTAGE apple, brioche, honey, nuts	**£££**
BLANC DE NOIRS VINTAGE red apples, berries, raspberry, almond	**£££**
BACCHUS FUMÉ NV+ green peas, passionfruit, elderflower	**££**
WEST DORSET CHARDONNAY VINTAGE+ light spice, melon, apricot blossom	**£**

Tours & tastings

Vineyard and Winery Tour, Grand Tour, Classic Tour (or Classic Winter Winery Tour) and in peak season the Summer Vineyard and Winery Grand Tour. Private tasting. Events: Nordic walking in the vines, visiting artists, wreath-making. Wine club. Harvest lunches. Dogs welcome but not in the winery.

Eating

Washingpool Farm can provide picnics; high season only, with tours or tastings.

Good to know

Castlewood Vineyard, Little Waddon Vineyard and Bride Valley are around thirty minutes away.

Langham Wine Estate

One of the most fêted wineries in the country

Of all the wineries that I was looking forward to visiting, Langham was at the very top of my list, because despite them having won a (frankly) ridiculous amount of plaudits, prizes and trophies over the last few years, I'd never actually tasted any of their wines and was itching to see what all the fuss was about. Their *prestige cuvée*, the Perpetual First Edition MV (multi-vintage) – made exclusively from Chardonnay – was awarded an unprecedented ninety-nine points at the 2025 WineGB Awards, as well as scooping up the title of Supreme Champion, Best Producer, Best Sparkling Wine, Best Premium Sparkling Wine, Best Blanc de Blancs, Best Blanc de Noirs, Best Non-Vintage Sparkling and the Regional Trophy for Wessex. They also won the 2025 IWSC Sparkling Wine Producer of the Year Award for a second time. The accolades are rolling in thick and fast.

The Langham family have been farming deep in the Dorset countryside for generations, and Justin Langham initially planted the classic three varieties – Chardonnay, Pinot Noir and Pinot Meunier – at Crawthorne Farm because he was inspired by his father's hobby vineyard nearby. Those initial plantings have increased with the huge success of the winery and there are now eighty-four acres under vine, largely grown on deep Cretaceous chalk.

The single-estate wines are made by 'wunderkind' winemaker Tommy Grimshaw, who took over the winemaking reins from Daniel Ham in 2019 and has continued to make wines following the low-intervention principles of smaller 'grower' – such as Anselme Selosse – as opposed to larger, more commercial Grandes Marques (for example, Moët & Chandon) Champagne. Although

many winemakers look for a neutral base wine for the second fermentation, Tommy explains that he wants character. They leave the grapes for longer on the vine to get them riper – so that the fruit can speak for itself – embrace oxygen, use wild as opposed to cultured yeasts, utilise old French oak for additional complexity in the base wine (they work with around 140 different components), and look for good acidity levels so that they can use less sulphur. Time under cork is as important – if not more so – than long lees ageing, dosage is low, as is the pressure of the bubbles; they have worked gently to make the wine rich and complex, and they don't want to mask the *terroir* with sugar. Simply put, Tommy says they are 'massive wine nerds' and want to 'make the best wines in the world'. They could very well be doing just that.

The Wines

In the Tasting Room, which used to be the old milking shed, there is an entire wall full of framed awards and certificates above a beautiful shelf bedecked with fairy lights and trophies. And despite there being a power cut during my time there, the wines really shone. It was like being in a vinous Aladdin's Cave, and whilst I wasn't surprised by the quality of these magical wines – that is a given – I was surprised by the prices. The Perpetual MV is understandably expensive, but the other wines are extremely good value, given the sheer brilliance of the liquid.

CORALLIAN CLASSIC CUVÉE NV*
spicy, apples, fresh, citrus, beguiling — £££

CULVER CLASSIC CUVÉE NV*
broad, rich, spiced cherries, nuts, long — £££

ROSÉ NV
delicate colour, cherry Bakewell, almonds, savoury **£££**

BLANC DE BLANCS NV
golden colour, apple crumble, noisette, spice **££££**

PERPETUAL MV*
serious, spicy, baked apple, textured, long **££££££**

Tours & tastings

The team at Langham 'love wine and love telling people about wine' and there are a number of touring options available, including a Self-Guided Tasting & Vineyard Walk, a Guided Tour and private tours. For the full Langham experience, book onto the Winemaker's Tour.

Eating

Smiths Kitchen – a shabby-chic space with concrete floors and wooden tables – offers local, seasonal food.

Good to know

Dogs are welcome and, unusually, both dogs and children are permitted on the tours.

Somerset

Saddle Goose

Garagiste-style low-intervention wines from Frome

The rather wonderfully named Saddle Goose comes from a nineteenth-century term which essentially means a 'fool': you wouldn't try and put a saddle on a goose and fly. And that is what many people thought Adam Collins was, wanting to set up a business making and selling English wine; that he was foolish to consider growing grapes in our wet, marginal climate and then wanting to craft them using natural, minimal-intervention methods. But that is exactly what he has done, and with huge success: the wines are delicious, energetic and exciting.

Before becoming a winemaker, Adam was an art director, and his beautiful, creative labels hint at that; they are inspired by tattoo artists to 'reflect quality, artistry, authenticity and depth'. But a migraine condition – not helped by staring at screens all day, coupled with a loathing of his commute, left him determined to seek a new career path. His mother was a chef and he had inherited her love of food as well as wine, nature and craft, and so he started studying with the WSET, completed an M.Sc. in viticulture and oenology in France, and worked vintages abroad.

Returning home, he was determined to create a sustainable, natural wine company, focusing on grapes that 'take care of the land', following regenerative and organic principles, and uses Pinot Noir, Solaris, Bacchus and some Chardonnay and Rondo, with the Frome winery being ready in 2024. The benefit of winemaking in England is that there are very few rules, which allows winemakers to experiment, to 'make the best out of what is grown and push boundaries to see what is possible from English grapes'. Adam uses natural yeast, doesn't fine or filter, and makes small adjustments only. Styles include a five-year lees-aged, low-dosage

Blanc de Noirs, a skin-contact Bacchus, a Col Fondo, a chillable red and cider, all made at his small winery in Somerset.

The Wines

Mouth-watering, low-intervention wines.

BLACK GOOSE BLANC DE NOIRS VINTAGE
spiced red apple, toast, nuts, raspberry **£££££**

SKINS BACCHUS VINTAGE+*
quince, apricot, textured, spice **££**

CHEEKY RED VINTAGE+
fragrant, pure, spice, cherry blossom, hawthorn **££**

Tours & tastings

Offering a 'real, authentic, interesting, intimate experience', tastings allow visitors to come and sit around the tanks and barrels for a 'rustic, small-producer vibe'. Saturday Cellar Wine Tastings or by appointment. Cellar door. Events: barrel tastings, pizza nights. Private events.

Eating

BYO. Monthly pizza nights. Cheese and charcuterie on request for functions.

Good to know

They are situated in a industrial yet creative space near the train station. Wraxall is half an hour away.

Wraxall Vineyard

Rustic luxe in fashionable Somerset

Even though the vineyard was first planted in 1974 by the Holmes family, it was only as part of a smallholding; the property was still primarily a pig farm with some sheep, cattle and now vines, with the wine being made in an old barn. Since then, the vines have changed hands a few times, being sold to opera singer Raimund Herincx as well as to a couple of hoteliers in 2007, who played a part in its rejuvenation before they put the vineyard up for sale.

It wasn't, therefore, until Lexa Hunt and husband David Bailey came onto the scene that Wraxall really got the love and attention that it deserved. The couple had bought Wraxall Lodge, a 200-year-old farmhouse located next to the vines, in 2018, and so when the vineyard came up for sale, despite knowing nothing about viticulture, they bought it with Dr Alistair Nesbitt at vineyard consultants Vinescapes confirming it was a good site: warm, due south and producing high-quality grapes. The following spring they planted the top field with Chardonnay and Pinot Noir, took out the Seyval Blanc, put further plantings of Chardonnay and Pinot Meunier in at the West Block and, on buying the orchard next door, more Pinot Noir and Pinot Noir Précoce. Bacchus is also grown and the site now totals fifteen acres.

Five wines are currently crafted from their fruit, two fizzes along with three still wines: two Bacchus (one is an oak-aged reserve) and a Pinot Noir Précoce rosé. The View, an utterly fabulous tasting room, restaurant, bar, event space and shop, was opened in 2023 with the specific aim of providing an outlet for these moreish, award-winning wines. Indeed, it is an outstanding spot, and I will forever remember my (rather windy) stay here, with the cosy yet stylish shepherd's hut more than a match for the gale outside, whilst eating the best cottage pie I have *ever* had!

The Wines

Wines are made off site at Itasca Wines.

CLASSIC CUVÉE VINTAGE
elegant, citrus, apples, almonds — £££

SPARKLING ROSÉ VINTAGE
delicate, raspberry pip, red apple — £££

BACCHUS VINTAGE+
pungent, white pepper, nettles, elderflower — £

Tours & tastings

Self-guided and guided wine tastings all year round from mid-week onwards. Vineyard tour and guided tastings run from spring to early autumn. Private tours. Pop-up events. Summer Sundays. Summer party. Wedding receptions.

Eating

The View@Wraxall is a superlative, child-friendly eaterie, wine bar and tasting room serving delicious local and seasonal food alongside a curated wine list. There is a plethora of options, including brunch, small plates, cheese and charcuterie, steak nights, Sunday lunch, monthly Land Rover pizzas, and fire cooking. The Nook is a delightful canvas-covered outside dining space.

Good to know

Accommodation is 'rustic luxury': the Old Winery Cottage No. 1 (sleeps two), the Old Winery Cottage No. 2 (sleeps four), Vine Cottage (sleeps eight) and two shepherd's huts. Saddle Goose, Fenny Castle Vineyard and Aldwick Estate aren't too far away. The Newt hotel and garden is close to nearby Bruton (as is Osip restaurant) and Frome is only half an hour away.

Devon

Lyme Bay Winery

A few years ago, Lyme Bay Winery sent me three of their top wines to try: two Pinot Noirs and a Chardonnay made from Martin's Lane Vineyard fruit. I tasted the wines and, frankly, was blown away. This was the very moment I realised that England was now making very, very good still wines; they were amongst the very best I had tasted that year.

The even more surprising thing, perhaps, was that the winery was arguably better known for making mead and fruit wines and yet these award-winning bottles were being crafted alongside quirkier and also more commercial offerings: Lyme Bay make 'white labels' for supermarkets. The top wines sell out fast, but you can visit the winery – based on an unshowy industrial estate in Devon – and taste a selection. Tastings only, no tours, as they buy their fruit in. Castlewood Vineyard is down the road and offers accommodation, tours, tastings and an annual wine festival.

Lympstone Manor Hotel

The five-star hotel with impressive wines and fine dining

Part of the illustrious Relais & Châteaux collection, Lympstone Manor is a Georgian, Grade-II-listed five-star country house hotel in Devon, owned by celebrity chef Michael Caines, that offers world-class food with delicious English wines. It also happens to occupy a truly uplifting spot; it's the sort of scenery that makes you stop in your tracks, take a breath and really look around to soak it all in, in particular the views over the vineyards to the sparkling Exe Estuary beyond.

Michael left two-Michelin-star Gidleigh Park – where he was head chef – to branch out on his own, and after a year of searching, he bought the property in September 2015 and knew immediately that he wished to plant a vineyard on the twenty-eight acres. And the wines, they were to emulate the very best French wines and be made in the style of Champagne, white and red Burgundy and Provence rosé.

Planting started in May 2018 and to classic French varieties only: three clones of Chardonnay, three of Pinot Noir and two of Pinot Meunier over a single vineyard of eleven acres. The site itself has an auspicious, south-facing microclimate and the warm body of water leads to mild springs and late summers. The tidal estuary isn't just beautiful, it has a fairly significant role to play in contributing both to the ripening of the grapes and mitigating against frost. Soils are sandy loam and clay over red Devon sandstone.

And the wines are excellent. The first vintage of Lympstone Manor Estate 'Triassac' Pinot Noir 2020 won a Gold Medal and the English Red Trophy at the 2023 International Wine Challenge.

The Wines

Made at Lyme Bay, these wines aren't cheap, but they are excellent. The Classic Cuvée NV is a red-grape-dominant blend, whilst the Edwards Chardonnay was named (as a surprise) after Steve Edwards, operations director and vineyard manager.

CLASSIC CUVÉE NV green apple, spice, citrus, beautiful balance	££££
EDWARDS CHARDONNAY VINTAGE+* spice, stone fruit, silky, textured, superb	££££
TRIASSIC PINOT NOIR VINTAGE+ expressive, fruit driven, red cherries, spice	£££

Tours & tastings
A vineyard tour for residents in high season, and lunch packages (the vineyard tour and lunch at the Pool House) for non-residents. Upgrades to various fine-dining experiences are also possible.

Eating
One of the best meals of my entire life, the Signature eight-course tasting menu, matched with estate (and other) wines, is simply stellar. This is fine dining at its very best with all dishes being expertly crafted to match their wines.

Good to know
There are twenty-one exquisite rooms with each named after a bird found on the estuary; the hotel's logo is a heron. Also six shepherd's huts near the vineyard, a tennis court, heated pool, and the Lady's Walk takes you through gardens peppered with sculptures. An extraordinary place.

Sandridge Barton

An idyllic rural setting close to the River Dart

This 450-acre family-owned estate was bought by the Moon family in the early 2000s, as they were looking for a country escape and the location was ideal; they are keen sailors, and it is near to both Dartmouth and the River Dart. Historically, the estate grew grapes, which they sold to Sharpham Wines - where vines were first planted in 1981 by Maurice Ash - but in 2020 the Sharpham Trust didn't renew the lease for the wine business, and so it moved across the river to its new home at Sandridge Barton.

Vineyards today total around forty acres and are planted on limestone with some slate and a shallow, sandy loam topsoil. Varieties include Chardonnay, Pinot Noir, Bacchus, Madeleine Angevine, Pinot Gris, Pinot Blanc and Sauvignon Blanc. Though they are not certified organic, chemicals such as insecticides and herbicides are not used, whilst potash (potassium) and bio-stimulants (such as seaweed) are utilised for fruit quality. Soil health and regenerative viticulture are promoted as much as possible.

Wines, under the careful direction of CEO and head winemaker Duncan Schwab (who started at Sharpham in 1992) and winemaker Charlie Brown, follow similar principles. There is a minimal-intervention or hands-off approach across all three of the ranges: the Dart Valley Series, the Single Vineyard Series and the wonderfully named Don't Feed the Ponies range. There are three different vineyard sites: Sandridge Barton, Stoneyfield and Reservoir Field, and the Don't Feed the Ponies wines are named after different tors (distinctive outcrops of granite rock) on Dartmoor, such as Little Bee. Alternative winemaking methods and styles are favoured, and as such they use *flor* and skin contact, with both traditional method and Col Fondo sparkling wines being made. All ferments are

spontaneous, they don't manipulate them, and only three of their larger-volume wines are fined. Minimal amounts of sulphur are used. The wines are so, so good; one-of-a-kind, original and joyful, they are a modern take on both the heritage varieties and French ones. Savour them in Sandridge Barton's stupendous guest centre, which is the embodiment of unpretentious winery cool.

The Wines

There is a large range of unique, delicious, experimental wines.

FIGGIE DANIEL COL FONDO VINTAGE
citrus, pineapple, floral — ££

CLASSIC CUVÉE VINTAGE*
nuts, spice, red apple, pecans — £££

LITTLE BEE VINTAGE+
tangerine, pithy, textured, grapefruit — ££

SONNY VINTAGE+*
pear, spice, *flor*, tangy, quince — ££

EAST FIELD PINOT NOIR VINTAGE+*
violets, red cherry, maraschino, blueberry — £££

Tours & tastings

Run all year, seven days a week. Self-guided (walk-ins) and guided wine tastings (includes a visit to the winery and two cheeses). Vineyard Safari (spring-summer). Vineyard Walk. Friday Flight Nights. Sunset Social Club. The Vine Room is a private events space. Exhibitions and artwork in the Gallery Bar. Music events. A tempting shop selling wine, local artisan produce and gifts.

Eating

ROAM is their (alpine-vibe) restaurant serving local, seasonal modern British dishes with a Basque influence, in the old milking parlour, open for lunch five days a week. Sunday roasts. Supper clubs. Guest chefs and pop-ups. Raclette night. Gallery Bar menu (croquettes, clams, cheese).

Good to know

Amazing parking barn! Also three properties: Sandridge Barton House, the Boathouse and the Lower Well Farmhouse. Dog- and child-friendly. Cycle track from Totnes. Torquay and the English Riviera is thirty minutes away.

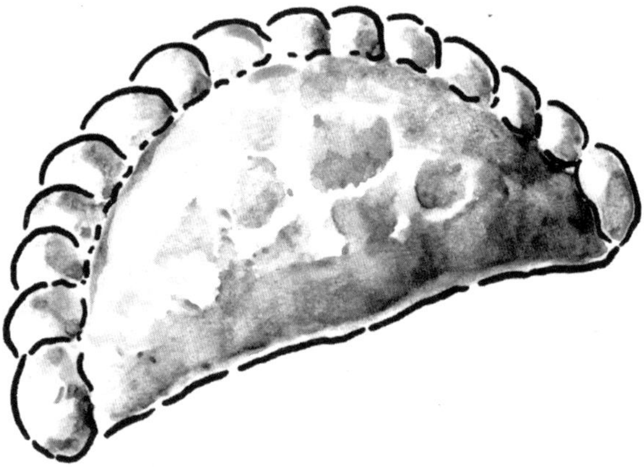

Cornwall

Camel Valley

The family-owned Cornish winery with two Royal Warrants

Camel Valley is one of the truly pioneering English family-owned wineries and one that is, rather wonderfully, now run by the second generation of the Lindo family – son Sam. A near-fatal plane crash during a training exercise led to RAF pilot Bob (aged thirty-six at the time of the accident) retiring from flying and in need of a new – and presumably – safer occupation. The popular TV show *All Creatures Great and Small* being filmed in Yorkshire from 1978 to 1980, where he and his wife, Annie, lived, meant they were priced out of any local farms in the area, which is how they found themselves moving down to Cornwall and becoming the proud owners of the worst sheep farm there; one so bad that it had been on the market for five years.

Sensibly, they decided to move the sheep on, and grew barley and potatoes instead, but couldn't help but notice that the south-facing slopes above the River Camel were a suntrap and found themselves wondering if vines would fare well there. Only one way to find out, and so in 1989 they planted 8,000 vines of Germanic varieties – Seyval Blanc, Triomphe and Reichensteiner – followed some years later by a few others, which included Dornfelder, Pinot Noir, Bacchus and Chardonnay, growing threefold to 16.5 acres. A winery followed and, knowing nothing about wine (apart from that they liked it, following a trip to France on their motorbike), Bob went to Germany to see how to process grapes and read a few books on how to make wine. They were ready to get started.

Rather serendipitously, this happened to coincide with the meteoric success of Rick Stein in Padstow, only half an hour away from their Bodmin base and the Lindo's delicate, award-winning sparkling and still wines pair wonderfully with the light, local fish dishes.

As well as being supported by local celebrity chefs, Camel Valley is the only winery in the country to have not one but two Royal Warrants (awarded to companies who regularly supply the Royal Household), for both the King and Queen of England, which has seen their wines served at state banquets and royal residences.

Despite their warrants, and being one of the first families to set up a serious wine business in England, Sam insists that they don't follow tradition, thinking of themselves as being more 'counterculture'. They don't use oak barrels, there is no extended lees ageing – they feel this is only really necessary for wines made from fruit grown on chalk soils and they prefer loam or slate for their own fruit and that from contract growers – no MLF and they don't neck-freeze their bottles when disgorging (freezing makes the yeast plug easier to remove), instead using the *à la volée* method: a manual disgorgement process where the bottle neck isn't frozen. Their wines have great acidity, minimal lees ageing and a fine mousse, which they believe is from the grapes being on the vine for a long time.

The wines are proudly Cornish, and Camel Valley have never tried to ape Champagne, originally only making still wines until an Italian winemaker suggested that they had great fruit for fizz. Today they make both styles, creating wines that they feel are truly unique and that can't be made anywhere else in the world. As if to prove this, they secured PDO status in 2017 for their Darnibole single vineyard, which produces a rather brilliant Bacchus.

The Wines

Camel Valley make a wide range of different styles but all tend to be light, fresh and elegant.

CORNWALL BRUT VINTAGE
lemon zest, honeysuckle, zingy acidity **£££**

PINOT NOIR ROSÉ BRUT VINTAGE*
lovely, cranberry, rosehip, raspberry **£££**

SPARKLING RED VINTAGE*
cassis, kirsch, raspberry **££**

BACCHUS DRY VINTAGE+
green peas, elderflower, pink grapefruit, zingy **£**

STILL CHARDONNAY VINTAGE+
spice, lemon, oatmeal **££**

STILL ROSÉ VINTAGE+
red fruits, red apple, cherry stones, peach skins **£**

Tours & tastings

The Lindo family understood and embraced the importance of hospitality fairly early on, being based in a tourist hotspot. Tasting room and cellar-door shop, daily guided tours during the week in the morning (closed at weekends) and a weekly Grand Tour & Tasting during high season, run by a winemaker. No dogs allowed.

Eating

Bar snacks only, but foodies are spoilt for choice with a lot of fantastic restaurants within a half-hour radius, including Barnaby's at Trevibban Mill.

Good to know

The Camel Trail runs at the bottom of the vineyard, Padstow is only thirty minutes away, and Polgoon Vineyard & Orchard is an hour away, in Penzance.

Trevibban Mill

Organic wines made in the Cornish countryside

Engin and Liz Mumcuoglu were bringing up their two sons in north London when in 2007 they viewed 6.5 acres of land in Cornwall that came with a ruined seventeenth-century watermill (which they initially planned to renovate), lake and woodland. This became their holiday home, and son Tom describes it as the 'pleasure land', as this was where they came to escape the city, ride quad bikes and enjoy being outdoors. When the fields next door were offered to them, they bought these too, and it was on this arable farmland that they first planted vines in 2008.

Whilst the idea at the beginning was to sell grapes, it wasn't long before they decided to make their own organic wine – both still and sparkling – and so they planted Reichensteiner, Dornfelder, Pinot Noir Précoce and Seyval Blanc. In 2023 more PIWIs were planted, including 1,500 vines of Sauvignac, some Pinotin and Souvignier Gris. Being organic, they use no herbicides, pesticides or fungicides, and even with the wet 2024 vintage there was no mildew in the PIWIs, which Tom describes as 'the future'. They also work with other organic or biodynamic partner sites for additional fruit.

Still wines – around 70 per cent – are the focus at Trevibban and Tom, who moved to Cornwall in 2018, is the winemaker for these whilst Salvatore Leone makes the fizz. They follow a minimum-intervention philosophy, meaning low sulphur, no fining and minimal filtration. Recently named the Best Producer in the South West at the WineGB West Awards, they make wines offering something for everyone, from brisk sparklings to skin contact, dry rosé and robust reds. The Southdown sheep that graze on the land also grace the labels.

The Wines

They love playing around with and creating new styles.

PINOT NOIR ROSÉ SPARKLING VINTAGE*
floral, raspberry, strawberries and cream £££££

HARLYN VINTAGE+
nettles, grapefruit, pineapple ££

ORION SKIN CONTACT VINTAGE+
amber, bitter orange, honeysuckle, nuts £££

DARK LANE RESERVE RED VINTAGE+
spice, pepper, cloves, plums, wow! £££££

Tours & tastings

All are guided. Tasting only, reserve tasting or a cider tasting. Tours include a Grand Walking Tour with a family member, usually Liz (high season), which includes a tasting and lunch. Guided tours are in the afternoon at weekends.

Eating

Excellent eaterie – Barnaby's – courtesy of the team behind the fabulous Prawn on the Lawn. Shop, deli and foodboard specials from the Winery Bar: grazing boards, charcuterie, dips, sweet treats. Cream teas.

Good to know

Two vineyard retreats (one bed) available: Cicero's Lodge (small dog allowed) and the Wine Maker's Lodge (no dogs). No kids in cabins. A range of CBD food products, Themptation, are available in the shop.

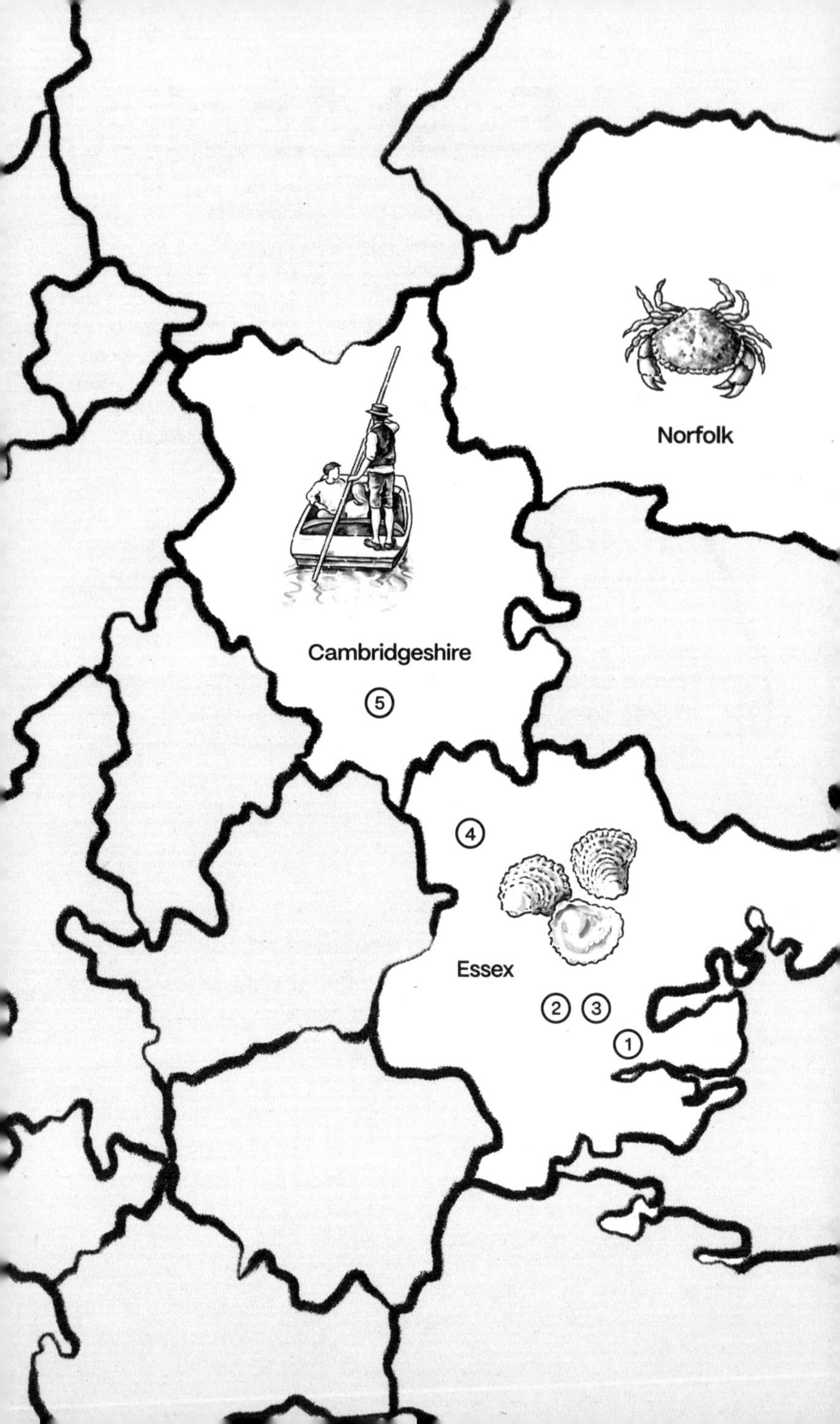
Norfolk
Cambridgeshire
5
4
Essex
2
3
1

East Anglia

A rather interesting thing has happened over the last few years, in that Essex – and the Crouch Valley in particular – has become something of the 'darling' of the English wine industry, with the warm climate, longer sunshine hours and clay soils working together to produce incomparably ripe fruit, ideal for still wines. Subsequently, some really fantastic wines (sparkling too) are being made here, and also in Cambridge and Norfolk, with all three shining a light on the extraordinary quality of wines that is now possible.

1. Crouch Ridge Estate
2. Danbury Ridge Wine Estate
3. New Hall Vineyards
4. Saffron Grange
5. Gutter & Stars
6. Flint Vineyard

Essex

Crouch Ridge Estate

A number of years ago a retailer I work with hosted an event at Crouch Ridge, where we tasted a selection of their English wines at the vineyard on the outside terrace. It was a baking hot weekend in the summer and the vista across the vines and down to the River Crouch was mesmerising. Visit for a Grand Tour & Tasting, a self-guided flight in their Wine Barn or indulge in a cream tea. There is also a great selection of platters and plates as well as onsite accommodation: six cottages (all two bed) and Mal's Barn for up to ten people.

Danbury Ridge Wine Estate

Danbury Ridge, one of the most prestigious of all English wineries, is slowly lifting the drawbridge. Whilst visits are not currently offered to the general public, they have a mailing list through which wine lovers can buy allocations of their esteemed wines, which can then be collected from the winery, with tastings running on those days. Wines are made by Liam Idzikowski, and his sensational sparkling wine, Solstice, is one of my favourite English fizzes. Still wines – both Estate and Block – are only made from Chardonnay and Pinot Noir.

New Hall Vineyards

East Anglia's pioneer producer

For years it was the chalky soils of the South and North Downs, from which sparkling wines reminiscent of Champagne could be made, that caused untold excitement in the industry, with producers gravitating to the likes of Kent, Sussex and Hampshire to set up shop. But now the Crouch Valley in Essex – this warm, dry little corner of East Anglia with long sunshine hours and clay soils – is coaxing unprecedented ripeness levels out of grapes. As a result, the still wines now being made in England are better than ever before, with some of the most prestigious wineries around the country sourcing Essex fruit for their wines.

And New Hall got here first, many decades ago, when Bill and Sheila Greenwood started their business back in 1969, being one of the first producers to make a traditional method English sparkling wine from Chardonnay and Pinot Noir. When they retired, it stayed within the family: Chris Trembath bought it from his brother-in-law Piers Greenwood (Bill and Sheila's son) in 2015, with his daughter Becki joining the team a year later. When they took over, around 50 per cent of their fruit was being sold elsewhere, but their vision was to concentrate on making more of their own wines.

Today they have 120 acres under vine (heritage, French and PIWI varieties) and a new winery was built in 2020 in time for the 2021 harvest. This was released under the New Hall Wine Estate brand rather than New Hall Vineyard, and their cellar door and tasting room – with roller doors, vineyard views and a small terrace – is a popular place to enjoy a glass of sparkling Bacchus.

The Wines

Affordable, approachable still wines are made, and both Charmat and traditional method sparkling wines.

RAILWAY BARN SPARKLING BACCHUS NV*
elderflower, herbal, fresh £££

CLASSIC CUVÉE BRUT NV
apple blossom, pear, citrus ££

SINGLE ESTATE PINOT NOIR PRÉCOCE ROSÉ VINTAGE+
watermelon, strawberry, floral £

Tours & tastings

Open-estate days in the summer. Limited tour and tasting dates in high season. Self-guided fourteen-point trail in the summer (map provided, dogs welcome). Social Saturdays (cellar door) spring to harvest. Self-guided wine flights. Cellar Door Collabs: pop-up food offerings on select weekends. Cellar-door shop. Vine leasing scheme.

Eating

Nibbles only, but you can bring your own picnic, or there is a local pub, the Purleigh Bell.

Good to know

Other producers nearby include Danbury Ridge (you can only visit if a customer), Missing Gate Vineyard and Crouch Ridge Estate – all around fifteen minutes. Also Crouch Valley Wine Tours.

Saffron Grange

Where woolly mammoths used to roam

This boutique, family-run winery was dreamt into life by Paul Edwards, who was a biochemist with a corporate food and drinks background. But he loved wine, drank a lot of it, studied for his WSET qualifications and 'wanted to have a bash at growing grapes'. In 2008 the lure to do that proved too strong and he planted a test vineyard, with further plantings following in 2011, 2018 and 2021 of the classic three varieties – Chardonnay, Pinot Noir and Pinot Meunier – as well as Pinot Gris and Seyval Blanc. Viticulture follows regenerative and sustainable principles, with there also being tree planting, rewilding, flower banks and composting.

The plan was always to produce single-vineyard sparkling wines that would showcase the *terroir* of their North Essex chalk soils and dry microclimate, with their first commercial vintage being 2016 and their own winery being finished in 2021. Wine labels are really striking, with a distinctive mammoth on them; tusks and teeth from woolly mammoths were discovered in the River Slade at the bottom of the site, and so the logo reflects the history of the land. Rather at odds with the prehistoric mammals found nearby, Saffron Grange are working with Queen Mary University London, Defra, Innovate UK and Extend Robotics, trialling robots who are controlled remotely to gently hand-pick grape bunches.

The tasting room and shop were opened at the same time as the winery, and Paul's son Nick and wife Aimee have created a really welcoming, inviting space – both inside and out – in which to relax and enjoy some of their fine Essex fizz.

The Wines

Made by Litmus winemaker Matthieu Elzinga; sparkling wines only.

THE REBEL BLANC DE GRIS VINTAGE*
floral, fresh, pear, nectarine, melon — ££

SEYVAL BLANC RESERVE VINTAGE
jasmine, honeysuckle, nuts, melon — £££

CLASSIC CUVÉE NV*
croissant, nuts, brioche — £££

SPARKLING ROSÉ VINTAGE
restrained, raspberry pip, sherbet, cherry blossom — £££

Tours & tastings

Available all year, with more availability in the summer. Try flights: self-guided tastings with three samples. Sundowner Fridays spring to summer; family-friendly. Mammoth Day Out in September. Harvest party.

Eating

Pre-order a cheese, charcuterie or seafood plate. Supper Clubs and weekly food trucks or seafood platters in high season.

Good to know

Gutter & Stars in Cambridge is around forty minutes away, as is Tuffon Hall, with Giffords Hall and Wyken Vineyard being slightly further afield. Topplesfield Vineyard offers luxurious accommodation.

Cambridgeshire

Gutter & Stars

The urban winery producing small parcels of stellar wines

Ex-music journalist Chris Wilson set up his characterful Cambridge urban winery in the basement of Chesterton Mill during the 2020 Covid pandemic, naming it after a beautiful, inspirational line from an Oscar Wilde play. In *Lady Windermere's Fan*, Lord Darlington proclaims that: 'We are all in the gutter, but some of us are looking at the stars.'

Galvanised by what he saw other like-minded people doing both in England and overseas, especially Blackbook in London and Savage Wines in South Africa, with his wife's encouragement, Chris made the move from writing about music to making wine. With no vineyard holdings of his own, he sources fantastic fruit from a handful of growers, primarily from nearby Essex and in particular the Crouch Valley: the Holy Grail of grapes.

Since starting out, Chris has made over thirty small parcels of wine, each with its own label and name, even if it is just from a different vintage. And the names are utterly brilliant, reflecting his love of music, wine and sense of humour: think Fizzee Rascal and Sparklife. These are the ultimate in boutique, low-intervention, gravity-fed wines, so popular that they sell out every year.

Even though he follows a very hands-off approach, as a Plumpton College graduate he keeps a strict eye on everything. All still whites are fermented and aged in old oak, Pinot Noir is open-top fermented (typically in stainless steel) and pressed into barrel, and sulphur levels are carefully watched, along with no fining or filtration. As Chris says, 'The shackles are off – why not experiment?' a feeling shared by a great number of the more experimental winemakers who appreciate the lack of strict rules and regulations in England's relatively new industry.

The Wines

These artisan, small-batch wines sell out fast, but I bought a couple of bottles 'for my husband' for Christmas.

SPARKLIFE COL FONDO VINTAGE
tropical, orange, pineapple £££

STAR 69 LONGPLAYER CHARDONNAY VINTAGE+
spice, toast, apricot, citrus £££

FADE INTO YOU PINOT NOIR VINTAGE+*
sappy, cherries, pure, delicious £££

Tours & tastings

Typically two tastings a month, with free open days every three months. The wine club is capped at one hundred members, who receive three bottles, three times a year. Private and corporate events.

Eating

Grab pizza at the Carpenters Arms at the end of the road, or try Restaurant 22 on Chesterton Road.

Good to know

Easy to reach by public transport. Saffron Grange is just over half an hour away.

Norfolk

Flint Vineyard

Get your geek on at this atmospheric Norfolk winery

You couldn't make up the fact that the original name of this memorable vineyard was Paradise Farm, first planted by founder and winemaker Ben Witchell in 2016, along with landowner Adrian Hipwell. The winery was built the same year, and whilst waiting for their own estate-grown fruit to come on stream, they bought some in to start making use of the space. The first five acres of their own vines were Bacchus, Pinot Blanc, Pinot Gris, Pinot Noir and Pinot Noir Précoce, with further plantings going in over the next few years. The popularity of their rosé and white Charmat method sparklers has also seen them put in hybrids and PIWIs such as Rondo, Solaris and Dornfelder.

The core range is comprised of the two dry sparkling wines as well as a red Précoce, a white Fumé and one of my favourite English whites, Silex, a lightly oaked blend of a number of different grape varieties that uses different winemaking techniques and vessels to create the desired wine. Labels are playful and distinctive: the colour of the circles reflects the flavour profile of the wines, and the two linked circles or Venn rings sees one circle represent the traditional way of making wines with the second meaning 'innovation'. Flint is found in the middle. The broad ethos at Flint is 'serious fun'; it's a place full of wine passion, where the wines are crafted and created in a really complex way but made to be approachable and enjoyable.

And they are now ready to show off their wines on site; there has been a real step change with regards to their hospitality offering. The walls are bedecked with fairy lights, there is a log burner and a cosy snug for the winter months, and plenty of outdoor seating for the summer. This is the ideal place to while away a weekend with a restorative glass of wine.

The Wines

The wines are fabulous; the almost neon-pink fizz and excellent still wines (including a new rosé) are all at accessible prices.

CHARMAT NV* pear, melon, elderflower, honeysuckle	££
CHARMAT ROSÉ NV* strawberry shoelaces, raspberry, rhubarb	££
FUMÉ VINTAGE+ grapefruit, elderflower, lime, peas	£
SILEX VINTAGE+* spice, oatmeal, textured, waxy	££

Tours & tastings

The cellar-door shop and wine bar are open during the week, and it's possible to drop in, taste and purchase wine. Tours and tastings run weekends only in the winter, with a wider offering in the summer. They can be quite nerdy – if you want them to be – so this is a great place to ask questions and learn. There are also weekly live-music nights and yoga in the barn.

Eating

Tapas-style sharing plates from the kitchen from spring to summer, along with pop-up food trucks and supper clubs. The wider area is a coastal, foodie haven.

Good to know

Flint is dog- and child-friendly, though they must be accompanied at all times. Winbirri Vineyard is about half an hour away.

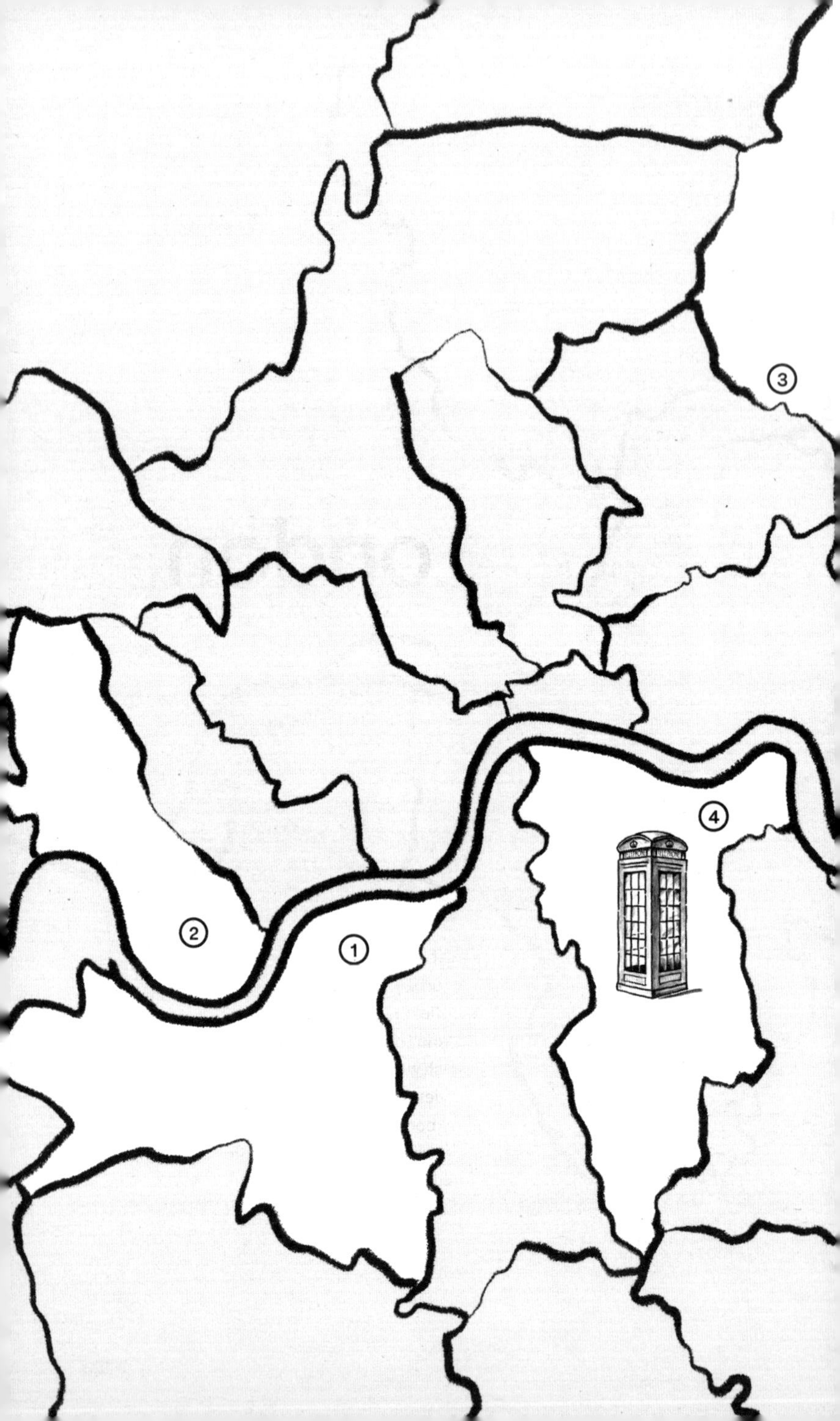
③
②
①
④

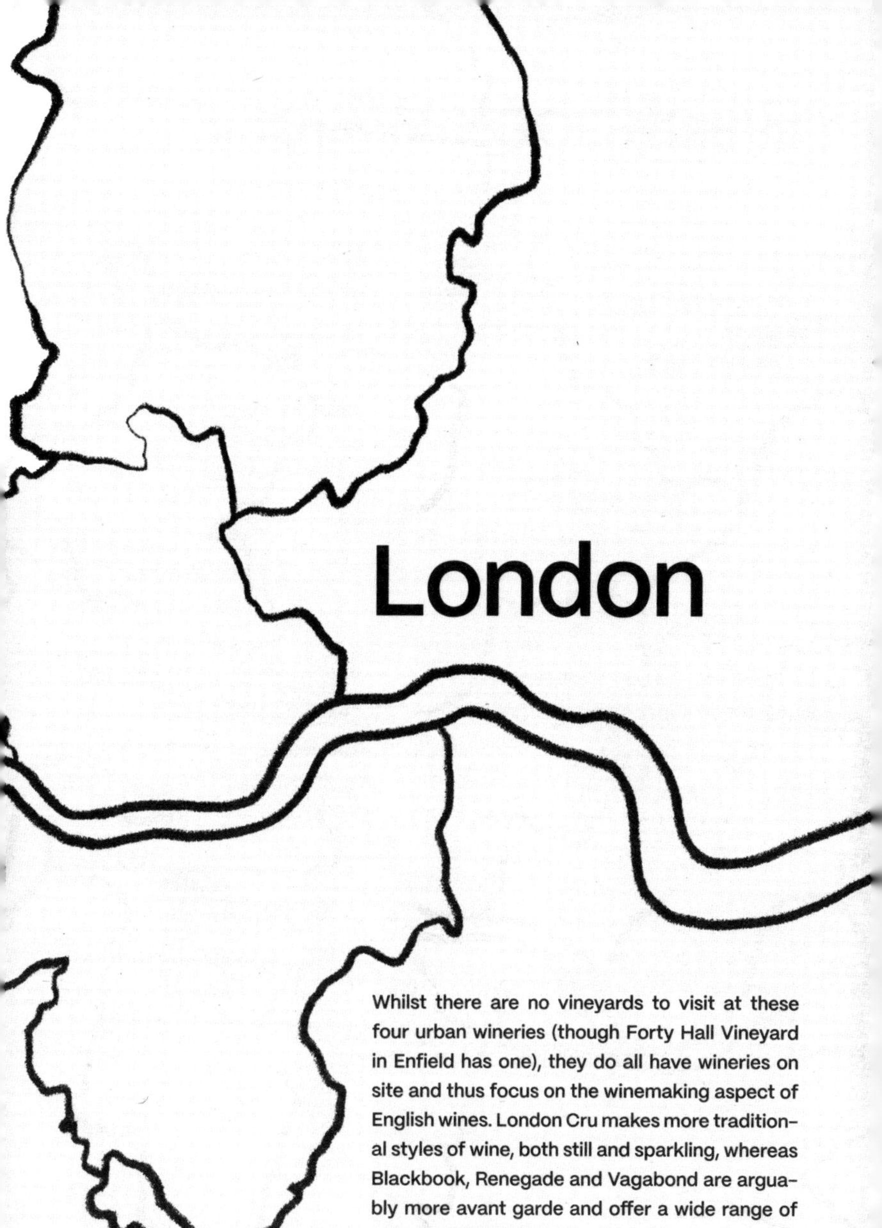

London

Whilst there are no vineyards to visit at these four urban wineries (though Forty Hall Vineyard in Enfield has one), they do all have wineries on site and thus focus on the winemaking aspect of English wines. London Cru makes more traditional styles of wine, both still and sparkling, whereas Blackbook, Renegade and Vagabond are arguably more avant garde and offer a wide range of eclectic wine styles.

1. Blackbook Winery
2. London Cru
3. Renegade Urban Winery
4. Vagabond Wines Urban Winery

Blackbook Winery

Battersea's urban winery showcasing low-intervention wines

On moving to London in the 1990s, American Sergio Verillo found a job as a sommelier and knew that he had found his calling working in the wine industry, one that would ultimately see him moving from serving wines to making them. In order to do this, he went to Plumpton College to study, and, on graduating, worked in many different countries around the world at a number of prestigious wineries before returning to England.

Keen to showcase his love of cool-climate Chardonnay and Pinot Noir, he set up urban winery (more prevalent at the time in the United States than in the United Kingdom) Blackbook with his wife Lynsey in 2017, in Battersea, working with his favourite varieties (and a few others) but focusing on still wines. All fruit is sourced from a two-hour radius around Blackbook, and Sergio only works with vineyards that he knows to be producing high-quality fruit. Indeed, the name Blackbook itself is a reference to him having a 'black book' of top grape growers.

Describing his wine style as 'inherently English with a touch of Connecticut', minimal intervention and wild yeasts are used where possible along with low sulphur levels. Wines are elegant, appealing and quite classic in style, juxtaposing pleasingly with the striking artwork on the outside of the bottles.

The Wines

Distinctive wines, with the labels all being a homage to London.

PAINTER OF LIGHT CHARDONNAY VINTAGE+*
spice, lemon, smart — ££

FRAGMENTS OF TIME SAUVIGNAC VINTAGE+
crisp, gooseberry, green, fresh — ££

NIGHTJAR PINOT NOIR VINTAGE+
fragrant, perfumed, floral, cranberry — ££

DRUMS>SPACE FIELD BLEND VINTAGE+
black cherry, chocolate, plums, spice — ££

Tours & tastings
Mostly run on weekends. The Blackbook Wine Bar opens in the summer (mid-spring to end-September) on weekends; tap-room vibe. DJ.

Eating
Nibbles. Some pop-ups.

Good to know
Open-door policy; kids and dogs welcome.

London Cru

The UK's first urban winery

When Cliff Roberson bought an empty Victorian warehouse – which used to be a gin distillery – for storage, next door to his eponymous wine business, little did he know that it would become the UK's first urban winery. But, travelling round the world for work, he found himself inspired by the goings-on in the likes of California and other urban wine centres, and converted the space into a winery in 2013, buying in grapes to make wine. London Cru was born.

At the age of eighty-two, not content with just buying in grapes, Cliff bought Foxhole in 2023, an 18.5-acre vineyard in West Sussex that borders Bolney Wine Estate. Already planted, the core varieties are Pinot Noir Précoce (their still red is dreamy and slightly reminiscent of a light Central Otago Pinot), Bacchus, Pinot Noir and Pinot Gris, with some Chardonnay too.

Once transported to the winery in London, London Cru make predominantly still wines but also some fantastic fizz, utilising a mix of winemaking vessels, including stainless-steel tanks and French oak barrels, but also concrete tanks and eggs (egg-shaped vessels). Australian winemaker Alex Hurley (ex-Gusbourne) has been here since 2018, and the wines are impressive.

The Wines

Wines are well made and varied, with Pét-Nats and traditional method fizz alongside still wines made from classic, hybrid and PIWI varietals.

VINTAGE BRUT*
nutty, broad, sourdough, apple tart — **£££**

BACCHUS VINTAGE+
lime zest, pink grapefruit, peach skin — **££**

PINOT NOIR PRÉCOCE VINTAGE+*
fragrant, red cherries, spice, plums — **££**

Tours & tastings

Welcome to the Winery tours tend to run a couple of times a month on set days and their Winemaker for the Day experience is monthly. Corporate events. Private hire.

Eating

A chef can be hired for events. Gastropub the Atlas is across the road; lunch here is included in the Winemaker for the Day session.

Good to know

As well as making wine, London Cru is a fabulous event space, where the Tank Room (maximum eighty people) and the cosier Barrel Room (a large central table can seat fifteen people, or twenty standing) can be hired or, indeed, the entire venue.

Renegade Urban Winery

The experimental winery in E17

Keen to do something a bit different in an industry that he loved, Warwick Smith switched careers, making his first wines at the original Bethnal Green location in 2016. Over time, though, Renegade outgrew that space (they still own the bar) and so in 2021 he established the Walthamstow winery in order to be able to increase production.

Historically, the wines being made weren't exclusively English, with fruit also coming in from Europe; countries such as France, Italy and Spain. But looking to the future, they want to make more English wines, still in particular, working with PIWIs and biodynamic fruit to create interesting and eclectic bottles for wine lovers to try.

Their philosophy is to make experimental wines, but also commercial ones, making a hopped (made with hops, like beer), sparkling English wine, a Col Fondo Rondo and a white Cabernet Sauvignon alongside crisp whites and lightly oaked Chardonnay. They don't want to make the same styles as everyone else and plan to 'embrace the niche', and their impressive winery space is just the place to try these eclectic wines. Choose from the bar and bistro on the mezzanine (the winery is on the ground floor) or take your bottle out to the south-west facing garden with canal views, or the large front terrace.

The Wines

Experimental wines with distinctive labels.

KAREN WHITE CABERNET SAUVIGNON VINTAGE+
cassis, crunchy, pomegranate — ££

ROGER COL FONDO RONDO VINTAGE
plums, black cherries, blackberries — ££

BETHNAL BUBBLES 3.2 DRY HOPPED NV
tropical, citrus, hoppy — ££

Tours & tastings

Once daily at weekends. Friday sees kid-friendly Pinot and Bambino sessions, complete with soft play. Live pianist. Seasonal events. Cheese and wine.

Eating

The kitchen serves British food 'with a winery twist'. Popular Sunday roasts.

Good to know

The Bethnal Green bar is open on specific weekdays as well as all weekend. Lots of breweries locally too, and other artisan drinks producers. Very inclusive and accessible. Dogs welcome.

Vagabond Wines Urban Winery

London's 'Cathedral of Wine'

American Stephen Finch set up the Vagabond business in 2010 to encourage wine exploration and experimentation before producing Vagabond's own wines, with the Canada Water Urban Winery (London's largest) opening in December 2025 and operating as a winery, bar and kitchen.

Whilst their own-label wines used to be made at the Battersea Power Station location, they are now made at Canada Water, and initial plans are to double production before scaling it up significantly over five years. The range comprises around ten wines, predominantly still, with a couple of sparklings, and all fruit is bought in (there are no vineyard holdings) from Kent, Oxfordshire, Suffolk, Sussex and the Crouch Valley. The wines are low intervention, with wild ferments, go through natural MLF and use minimal sulphur, with no fining or filtration.

As with the other bars in the Vagabond group, there is an impressive range of wines available to try at Canada Water, which showcases and celebrates other English wines too, from a rotating roster of producers such as Yotes Court, the Heretics, Whitewolfe and Danbury Ridge, as well as other London urban wineries. Believing that a 'rising tide lifts all ships', they want to be a 'Cathedral of Wine', serving different bottles from all over the country with a mix of styles and narratives so as to rightly cement their position as a hub for wine lovers, enthusiasts and the trade alike.

The Wines

Vagabond's thrilling own-label wines are made by José Quintana.

ORTEGA SOLENA BATCH 004 MV+ tropical fruits, jasmine, bitter orange	£££
ORTEGA VINTAGE+ quince, honeysuckle, pear	££
DIOS MIO BACCHUS VINTAGE+ nettles, textural, spice, apple	££
CHARDONNAY VINTAGE+* spice, stone fruits, lemon	££
ROSÉ VINTAGE+* pale, juicy strawberry, raspberry, cherry	££

Tours & tastings
Run multiple times a weekend. The Vagabond Wine Academy is a WSET provider for level 1 and 2. Masterclasses. Cheese and wine. Winemaker dinners.

Eating
Wide range of small plates, sharing plates and boards, and nibbles.

Good to know
For other any padel addicts, there are four courts across the road at Instantpadel for a pre-tasting hit!

Index

Acknowledgements

A million thanks to everyone in this incredible industry who spared the time to chat to me, show me around and taste frankly bloody brilliant wines with me. This book is testament to you all. Thanks, too – as ever – to my hugely supportive and all-round amazing agent Hannah Schofield at LBA Literary Agency and to the wondrous team at Bloomsbury: Grace Paul and Emily North. Thanks to the wider book and creative team, too: Luke Bird, Carmen Balit, Claire Littlejohn and Kate Quarry. Finally, a big thank you to my family, especially my husband, Ed, who is a tower of strength, picking up the slack when needed when I'm in the writing zone. Wilf, you are of course absolutely no help at all, but as you know, I love you both immensely!

About the Author

Sam Caporn has been in the wine trade for her whole working life – over thirty years – and became a Master of Wine in 2011, winning the prestigious Madame Bollinger Award for Excellence in Tasting. She wrote her dissertation on English sparkling wines, used to be the English wine buyer for Direct Wines, and is the International Wine Challenge GB co-chair and a freelance wine consultant. This is her second wine book.